INDIANA

SCIENCE

FUSion

fusion [FYOO • zhuhn] a mixture or blend formed by fusing two or more things

This Interactive Student Edition belong

_____

Teacher/Room

_____

HOUGHTON MIFFLIN HARCOURT

HOUGHTON MIFFLIN HARCOURT

Front Cover: *green anole* ©Jeremy Woodhouse/Photodisc/Getty Images; *prism* ©Larry Lilac/Alamy; *clownfish* ©Georgette Douwma/Photographer's Choice/Getty Images; *galaxy* ©Stocktrek/Corbis; *ferns* ©Mauro Fermariello/Photo Researchers, Inc.

Back Cover: *robotic arm* ©Garry Gay/The Image Bank/Getty Images; *thermometer* ©StockImages/Alamy; *astronaut* ©NASA; *moth* ©Millard H. Sharp/Photo Researchers, Inc.

ISBN 978-0-547-43852-8

5 6 7 8 9 10 0877 19 18 17 16 15 14 13 12

4500357222   BCDEFG

Consulting Authors

Michael A. DiSpezio
Global Educator
North Falmouth, Massachusetts

Marjorie Frank
Science Writer and Content-Area Reading
Specialist
Brooklyn, New York

Michael Heithaus
Director, School of Environment and Society
Associate Professor, Department of Biological
Sciences
Florida International University
North Miami, Florida

Donna Ogle
Professor of Reading and Language
National-Louis University
Chicago, Illinois

Program Advisors

Paul D. Asimow
Professor of Geology and
Geochemistry
California Institute of Technology
Pasadena, California

Bobby Jeanpierre
Associate Professor of Science
Education
University of Central Florida
Orlando, Florida

Gerald H. Krockover
Professor of Earth and Atmospheric
Science Education
Purdue University
West Lafayette, Indiana

Rose Pringle
Associate Professor
School of Teaching and Learning
College of Education
University of Florida
Gainesville, Florida

Carolyn Staudt
Curriculum Designer for Technology
KidSolve, Inc.
The Concord Consortium
Concord, Massachusetts

Larry Stookey
Science Department
Antigo High School
Antigo, Wisconsin

Carol J. Valenta
Senior Vice President and Associate
Director of the Museum
Saint Louis Science Center
St. Louis, Missouri

Barry A. Van Deman
President and CEO
Museum of Life and Science
Durham, North Carolina

Power Up with Science Fusion!

Your program fuses . . .

Online Virtual Experiences

Hands-on Explorations

Active Reading

. . . to generate new science energy for today's science learner—*you*.

Active Reading

Be an active reader and make this book your own!

You can write your ideas, answer questions, draw graphs, make notes, and record your activity results right on these pages.

By the end of the school year, this book becomes a record of everything you learn in science.

Amph
or Rep

How are amphibians and reptiles different?
Read on to learn about these two groups.

tive Reading As you read these two pages, draw circles around
the words that signal when things are being compared.

Amphibians [am•FIB•ee•...]

...amphibians have smooth, moist ...kin. Young amphibians have gills. ...ny adult amphibians have lungs. ...ptiles are animals with scales covering their bodies. Lizards and turtles are reptiles. Similar to amphibians, most reptiles hat... from eggs. A reptile ... lungs its wh... crocodiles, th... water must c...

...amphibian li... round water.

...rtle

...ptile lays eggs.

Newts la... water.

Frille Lizar

Frilled lizard lay their egg the ground.

Hands-on Explorations

Science is all about doing.

There are lots of exciting investigations on the Inquiry Flipchart.

Ask questions and test your ideas.

Draw conclusions and share what you learn.

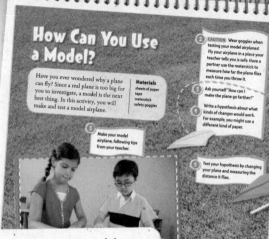

How Can You Use a Model?

Have you ever wondered why a plane can fly? Since a real plane is too big for you to investigate, a model is the next best thing. In this activity, you will make and test a model airplane.

Materials
sheets of paper
tape
meterstick
safety goggles

Make your model airplane, following tips from your teacher.

CAUTION: Wear goggles when testing your model airplanes! Fly your airplane in a place your teacher tells you is safe. Have a partner use the meterstick to measure how far the plane flies each time you throw it.

Ask yourself "How can I make the plane go farther?"

Write a hypothesis about what kinds of changes would work. For example, you might use a different kind of paper.

Test your hypothesis by changing your plane and measuring the distance it flies.

A Word for the W...
When you test a hypothesis, change only one thing at a tim... one thing is called the variabl...

Online Virtual Experiences

Explore cool labs and activities in the virtual world—where science comes alive and you make it happen.

See your science lessons from a completely different point of view—a digital point of view.

Science Fusion is new energy... just for YOU!

Contents

PROCESS STANDARDS
Nature of Science

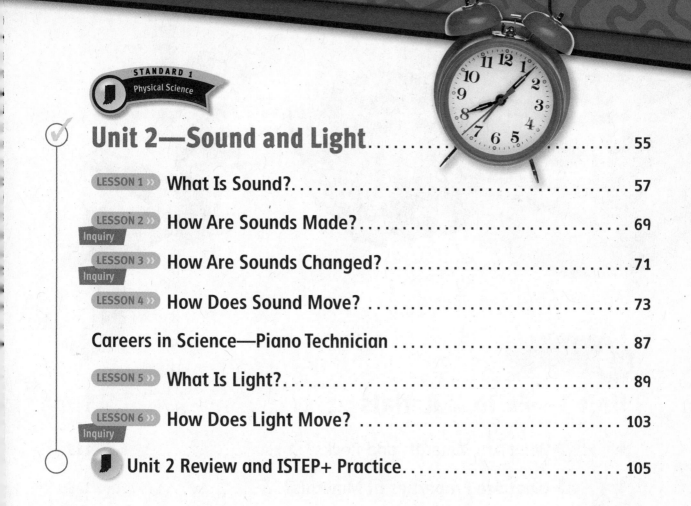

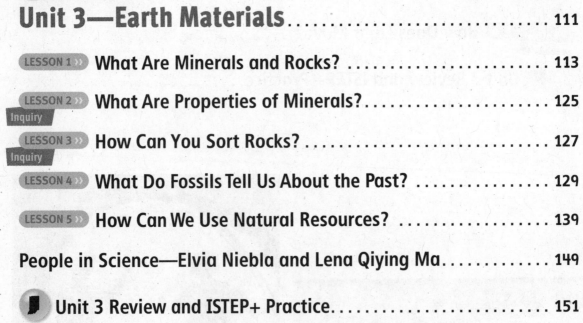

STANDARD 2
Earth Science

Unit 4—Plants

STANDARD 3
Life Science

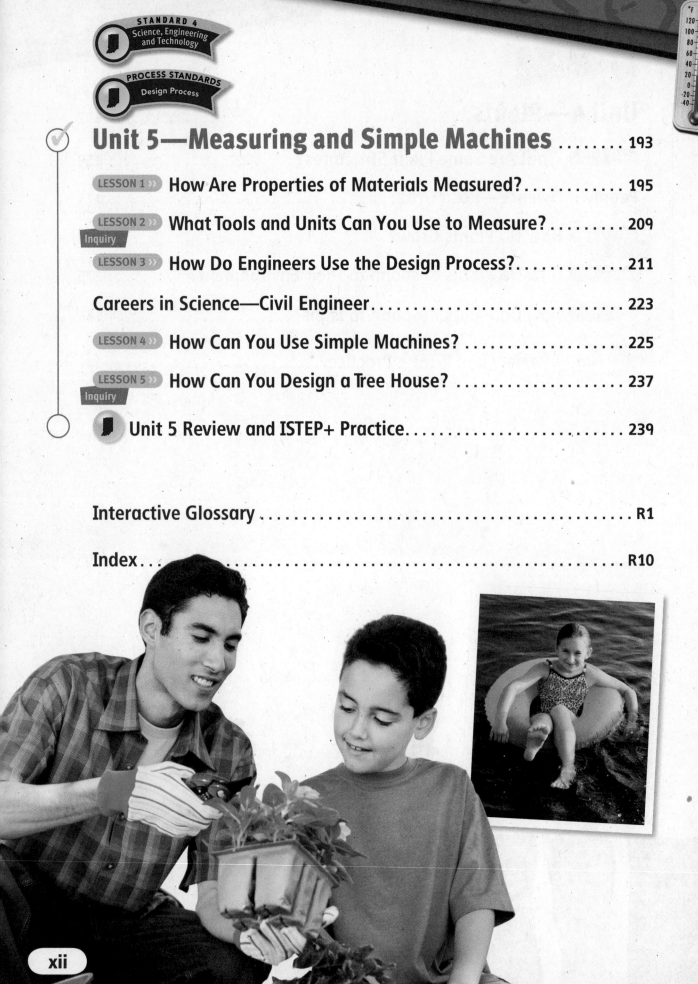

Unit 5—Measuring and Simple Machines 193

Scientists at Work

PROCESS STANDARDS
Nature of Science

Scientist at Purdue University

I Wonder Why

This scientist is working in a lab.
I wonder what tools and methods he uses.
Turn the page to find out.

Here's Why Scientists in Indiana use many tools to help them with their investigations. They use tools such as microscopes and petri dishes.

Track Your Progress

Essential Questions and Indiana Standards

PROCESS STANDARDS
Nature of Science

Students gain scientific knowledge by observing the natural and constructed world, performing and evaluating investigations and communicating their findings. These principles should guide student work and be integrated into the curriculum along with the content standards on a daily basis.

Nature of Science Students gain scientific knowledge by observing the natural and constructed world, rming and evaluating investigations and communicating their findings. These principles should guide ent work and be integrated into the curriculum along with the content standards on a daily basis.

Lesson 1

sential Question

low Do Scientists nvestigate Questions?

Engage Your Brain!

Find the answer to the following question in this lesson and record it here.

How is this student acting like a scientist?

_____

_____

_____

Active Reading

esson Vocabulary

ist each term. As you learn about each, make otes in the Interactive Glossary.

_____ _____

_____ _____

_____ _____

_____

Use Headings

Active readers preview, or read, the headings first. Headings give the reader an idea of what the reading is about. Reading with a purpose helps active readers understand what they are reading.

What Is Science?

Science is about Earth and everything beyond it. What does a scientist look like? To find out, take a look in the mirror!

As you read these two pages, underline the main idea.

Why do volcanoes erupt?

Look for a Question

How does a butterfly use its six legs? What does the shape of a cloud tell about the weather? It's never too soon to start asking questions! Write your own question below.

_____

_____

Science is a way of looking at the world and thinking about it. When you think like a scientist, you ask questions about the world around you. You try to answer your questions by doing investigations.

Some investigations are simple, such as watching animals play. Other investigations take planning. You need to gather and set up materials. Then you write down what happens.

You can think like a scientist on your own or in a group. Sharing what you learn is part of the fun. So get started!

Why does a compass point north?

What do stars look like through a telescope?

What Do You See?

So you want to think like a scientist? Let's get started. Try making some observations and inferences!

Active Reading As you read these two pages, find and underline the definition of *observe*.

Look at the pictures on this page. What do you see? When you use your senses to notice details, you **observe**.

Things you observe can start you thinking. Look at the picture of the small sailboat. You see that it has more than one sail. Now look more closely. The sails are different shapes and sizes.

You might infer that the shape or size of the sails affects how the boat moves. When you **infer**, you offer an explanation of what you observed. You might infer that each sail helps the boat move in a different way.

Make an observation about this boat.

_____

_____

_____

Make an observation about this ship.

_____

_____

CONTAINER SHIP

Make an observation about this boat.

_____

_____

623   U.S. COAST GUARD

Write an inference based on this observation:
"I can see the wind blowing this sail."

_____

_____

Getting Answers!

People ask questions all day long. But not all questions are science questions. Science questions can be answered in many ways.

As you read these two pages, circle a common, everyday word that has a different meaning in science.

Exploring

Some science questions can be answered by exploring. Say you see a leaf float by on the water. You wonder what else can float on water. You find an eraser in your pocket. You **predict**, or use what you know to tell if it will sink or float. When you know which items float and which don't, you can **classify**, or group, them.

Predict

Think about each item pictured. Then circle the ones you predict will float. Mark an X on those you predict will sink.

8

Investigating

You might think of an investigation as looking for clues. In science, an **investigation** is a planned way of finding answers to questions. When you do an investigation, you might ask a cause-and-effect question, "Does the amount of weight in a boat affect whether it floats or sinks?" Because you don't want to use a real boat, you can **make and use models.** A raft made of sticks is not exactly like a real boat, but it can be used to learn about them.

9

Investigating Answers

There are many steps a scientist may take during an investigation. Some do all five described here.

Active Reading As you read these two pages, number the sentences that describe Onisha's experiment to match the numbered steps in the circles.

1 Ask a Question

What causes things to change? This is the kind of question you can answer with an investigation.

2 Hypothesize

A **hypothesis** is a statement that could answer your question. You must be able to test a hypothesis.

Predict and Plan an Investigation

Predict what you will observe if your hypothesis is correct. **Identify the variable** to test, and keep other variables the same.

3

What Onisha Did ...

Onisha thought about rafts floating down a river. She asked a question, "Does the size of a raft affect the amount of weight it can carry?"

Onisha **hypothesizes** that a bigger raft can carry more weight. Then she predicted, "I should be able to add more weight to a bigger raft than to a smaller raft." Onisha planned an investigation called an experiment. Outside of science, experimenting means trying something new, such as a new recipe. In science, an **experiment** is a test done to gather evidence. The evidence might support the hypothesis, or it might not. In her experiment, Onisha built three model rafts that differed only in their number of planks. She carefully put one penny at a time onto each raft until it sank. She recorded her results and drew a conclusion.

Variable

The factor that is changed in an experiment is called a **variable**. It's important to change only one variable at a time.

Draw Conclusions

Analyze your results, and **draw a conclusion.** Ask yourself, "Do the results support my hypothesis?" Share your conclusion with others.

4 Experiment

Now do the experiment to test your hypothesis.

5

▶ What was the variable in Onisha's experiment?

_____

_____

Sum It Up!

When you're done, use the answer key to check and revise your work.

Write words from the lesson that match the pictures.

The small plane will fly farther.

1. _____

2. _____

3. _____

4. _____

Use what you learned from the lesson to fill in the sequence below.

observe → 5. _____

6. _____ → 7. _____

Name _____

Word Play

1 Use the words in the box to complete the puzzle.

Across

1. You do this when you make a conclusion after observing.
5. the one factor you change in an experiment
6. to make a guess based on what you know or think
8. something that is like the real thing—but not exactly
9. a statement that will answer a question you want to investigate

Down

1. Scientists plan and carry one out to answer their questions.
2. Scientists ask these about the world around them.
3. You do this when you use your five senses.
4. an investigation in which you use variables
7. You draw this at the end of an investigation.

experiment*   infer*   questions   investigation*   variable*   hypothesis*

predict*   model   observe*   conclusion

*Key Lesson Vocabulary

Apply Concepts

2 This bridge is over the Mississippi River. List materials you could use to make a model of it.

_____

_____

3 Greyson wants to know what plants need in order to survive. He places one plant in a window. He places another plant in a dark closet. What is the variable he is testing?

_____

4 Jared looks carefully at a young turtle in his hand. Label each of his statements _observation_ or _inference_.

Its front legs are longer than its back legs. _____

It has sharp toenails. _____

It uses its toenails to dig. _____

It can see me. _____

Its shell feels cool and dry against

my hand. _____

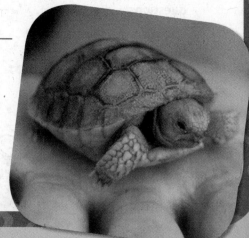

Take It Home! Share what you have learned about observations and inferences with your family. With a family member, make observations and inferences about items in or near your home.

The **Nature of Science** Students gain scientific knowledge by observing the natural and constructed world, performing and evaluating investigations and communicating their findings. These principles should guide student work and be integrated into the curriculum along with the content standards on a daily basis.

Name _____

Essential Question

How Can You Use a Model?

Set a Purpose

What is the question you will try to answer with this investigation?

_____

_____

_____

State Your Hypothesis

Write your hypothesis, or idea you will test.

_____

_____

_____

Think About the Procedure

What is the variable you plan to test?

_____

_____

How will you know whether the variable you changed worked?

_____

_____

Record Your Results

Fill in the chart to record how far the plane flew each time you changed its design.

Change Made to the Model	Distance It Flew

Draw Conclusions

1. Which changes to your model worked best?

_____

_____

_____

_____

2. Was your hypothesis supported by the results? How do you know?

_____

_____

_____

Analyze and Extend

1. How is your model the same as a real airplane?

_____

_____

_____

2. What did you learn about real airplanes from using a model?

_____

_____

_____

3. How is your model different from a real airplane?

_____

_____

_____

_____

_____

4. What can't you learn about real airplanes by using a paper airplane?

_____

_____

_____

_____

_____

5. Think of another question you would like to answer about airplane models.

_____

_____

_____

_____

Essential Question

How Do Scientists Use Tools?

Engage Your Brain!

A hand lens can make a bug look bigger.

What other tools make objects look bigger?

_____

_____

_____

Active Reading

Lesson Vocabulary

List each term. As you learn about each one, make notes in the Interactive Glossary.

_____

_____

_____

Compare and Contrast

Ideas in parts of this lesson explain comparisons and contrasts—they tell how things are alike and different. Active readers focus on comparisons and contrasts when they ask questions such as, How are measuring tools alike and different?

Make It Clear!

Scientists use tools to give them super-vision!
Some tools that do this include hand lenses
and microscopes.

Active Reading As you read these two
pages, circle words or phrases that signal
when things are alike and different.

Light microscopes let you see
tiny objects by using a light
source and lenses or mirrors
inside the microscope.

A magnifying box
has a lens in its lid.

A hand lens has one
lens with a handle.

Use forceps to pick up tiny objects
to view with magnifiers.

Use a dropper to move small
amounts of liquids for viewing.

Close, Closer, Closest!

Magnifying tools make objects look larger. Hold a hand lens close to one eye. Then move the hand lens closer to the object until it looks large and sharp. A magnifying box is like a hand lens in that it also has one lens. You can put things that are hard to hold, such as a bug, in it.

A **microscope** magnifies objects that are too tiny to be seen with the eye alone. Its power is much greater than that of a hand lens or magnifying box. Most microscopes have two or more lenses that work together.

▶ Draw a picture of how something you see might look if it was magnified.

Pond water as seen with just your eyes.

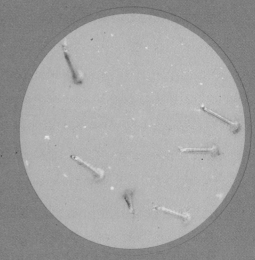

Pond water as seen through a hand lens.

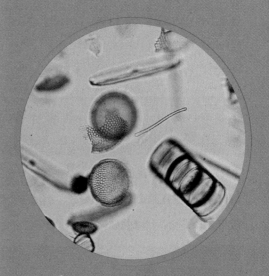

Pond water as seen through a microscope.

Measure It!

Measuring uses numbers to describe the world around you. There are several ways to measure and more than one tool or unit for each way.

Active Reading As you read the next page, circle the main idea.

A balance has a pan on either side. Put the object you want to measure on one pan and add masses to the other pan until they are balanced. The basic unit of mass is the gram.

The units on measuring tapes can be centimeters and meters or inches and feet.

ruler

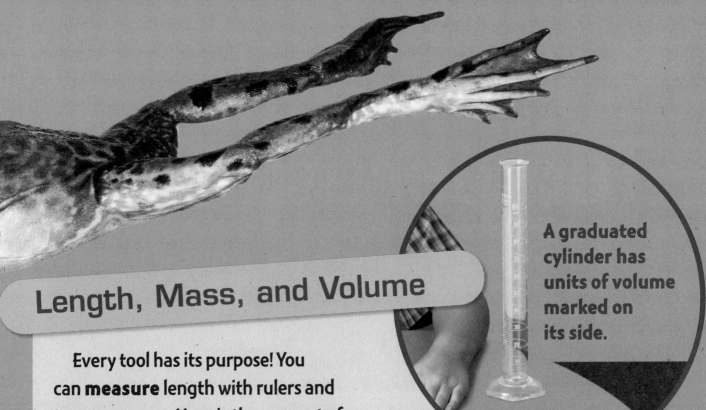

Length, Mass, and Volume

A graduated cylinder has units of volume marked on its side.

Every tool has its purpose! You can **measure** length with rulers and tape measures. Mass is the amount of matter in an object. It is measured with a pan balance. Volume is the amount of space a solid, liquid, or gas takes up.

The volume of a liquid can be measured with a **graduated cylinder** or a measuring cup or spoon. You can also use these tools to find the volume of solids that can be poured, such as sugar or salt. You **use numbers** to report measurements and **compare** objects. You can also **order** things using measurements. You can put pencils in order from shortest to longest.

Measuring cups and spoons are used because the amount of each ingredient is very important.

Do the Math!
Subtract Units

Use a metric ruler to measure the parts of the frog.

1. How many centimeters is the frog's longest front leg?

_____

2. How many centimeters is the frog's longest back leg?

_____

3. Now find the difference.

_____

4. Compare your measurements to those of other students.

_____

_____

Time and Temperature

How long did that earthquake shake? Which freezes faster, hot water or cold water? Scientists need tools to answer these questions!

Time

When you count the steady drip of a leaky faucet, you are thinking about time. You can **use time and space relationships.** Clocks and stopwatches are tools that measure time. The base unit of time is the second. One minute is equal to 60 seconds. One hour is equal to 60 minutes.

What if frogs held swim races across a pond? Here two frogs are racing.

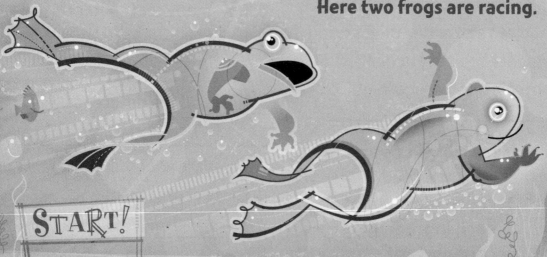

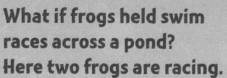

START!

Temperature

When you say that ovens are hot or freezers are cold, you are thinking about **temperature**. A thermometer is the tool used to measure temperature. The base units of temperature are called degrees, but all degrees are not the same.

Scientists usually measure temperature in degrees Celsius. Most people around the world use Celsius, too. In the United States, however, degrees Fahrenheit are used to report the weather, body temperature, and in cooking.

▶ The first frog finished the race in 19 seconds. The second frog finished the race in 47 seconds. How much more quickly did the winning frog finish the race?

_____

_____

_____

How Do You Care for Tropical Fish?

To care for tropical fish, you have to think like a scientist and use science tools.

Close Encounters

A public aquarium [uh•KWAIR•ee•uhm] is the place to see sharks and tropical fish. That's where many people get excited about keeping tropical fish at home. The word *aquarium* is used for both the big place you visit and the small tank in your home. Caring for both takes similar skills: observing, inferring, measuring, and recording data.

Does moving your aquarium in front of the window change the water's temperature?

What is the volume of water in your aquarium?

Keep Good Records

Keeping good records is important, whether you're recording data in your science notebook or making entries in your aquarium log. In your log, record the temperature every time you check it. Write the time you feed the fish and the volume of food you give them. Making correct measurements is part of being a good scientist.

Water test kits identify materials in the water.

Taking care of fish means checking the temperature.

Cause and Effect

Every change in an aquarium has a cause. Sometimes fish in an aquarium might become sick. Think of two things that might cause the fish to get sick.

_____

_____

_____

Sum It Up!

When you're done, use the answer key to check and revise your work.

The idea web below summarizes this lesson. Complete the web.

How Scientist Use Tools

1 They use hand lenses and microscopes to make things look _____.

They use tools to measure.

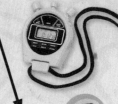

2 Length is measured with _____ _____.

3 A graduated cylinder measures _____.

4 Pan balances measure _____.

5 They measure time with clocks and _____.

Answer Key: 1. bigger, 2. rulers and measuring tapes, 3. volume, 4. mass, 5. stopwatches

Name _____

Word Play

1 Write each term after its definition. Then find each term in the word search puzzle.

A. A tool used to measure mass _____

B. A temperature scale used by scientists _____

C. A tool used to pick up tiny objects _____

D. A tool used to measure volume _____

E. A tool you hold against your eye to make objects look bigger _____

F. How hot or cold something is _____

G. A tool that measures temperature _____

H. Something you measure with a stopwatch _____

I. How much space something take up _____

```
L  T  E  M  P  E  R  A  T  U  R  E  R  M  Y  O  L
U  H  R  P  A  M  I  L  C  E  L  S  I  U  S  V  W
K  E  E  A  V  S  U  N  B  O  W  L  M  A  X  Y  M
N  R  V  N  U  O  M  Z  O  O  L  I  S  S  T  F  O
G  M  C  B  E  U  L  I  H  T  M  A  Y  T  L  O  K
Y  O  Y  A  B  L  U  U  M  I  M  M  Y  O  R  R  J
F  M  S  L  K  K  Z  W  M  M  X  Q  I  P  Z  C  D
K  E  H  A  R  O  O  R  L  E  A  F  S  I  M  E  E
E  T  N  N  R  U  C  L  M  K  P  I  U  T  X  P  H
S  E  N  C  F  I  L  L  H  A  N  D  L  E  N  S  S
J  R  U  E  M  M  U  V  L  V  I  G  T  H  M  I  T
G  R  A  D  U  A  T  E  D  C  Y  L  I  N  D  E  R
```

Apply Concepts

In 2–5, tell which tool(s) you would use and how you would use them.

thermometer

measuring
spoons

measuring
tape

ruler

magnifying box

2 Find out how long your dog is from nose to tail.

_____

_____

_____

3 Decide if you need to wear a sweatshirt outdoors.

_____

_____

_____

4 Make a bubble bath that has just the right amount of bubbles and is not too hot or too cold.

_____

_____

_____

_____

5 Examine a ladybug and count its legs without hurting it.

_____

_____

_____

_____

Take It Home!

Share what you have learned about measuring with your family. With a family member, identify examples of objects you could measure in or near your home.

The Nature of Science Students gain scientific knowledge by observing the natural and constructed world, performing and evaluating investigations and communicating their findings. These principles should guide student work and be integrated into the curriculum along with the content standards on a daily basis.

Name _____

Essential Question

How Can You Measure Length?

Set a Purpose
What will you be able to do at the end of this investigation?

_____

_____

_____

_____

Think About the Procedure
What will you think about when choosing the measurement tool for each item?

_____

_____

_____

How will you choose the units that are best for each item?

_____

_____

Record Your Results
In the space below, make a table in which you record your measurements.

Draw Conclusions

1. How does choosing the best tool make measuring length easier?

_____

_____

_____

_____

2. How do units affect the quality of a measurement?

_____

_____

_____

Analyze and Extend

1. Did groups who used the same tools as your group get the same results as you? Explain why or why not.

_____

_____

_____

2. Why was it important to communicate your results with other groups? Explain.

_____

_____

_____

3. When would someone want to use millimeters to find out who throws a ball the farthest? When would using millimeters not be a good choice? (1,000 mm = 1 m)

_____

_____

_____

4. Think of another question you would like to ask about measuring.

_____

_____

_____

© Houghton Mifflin Harcourt Publishing Company

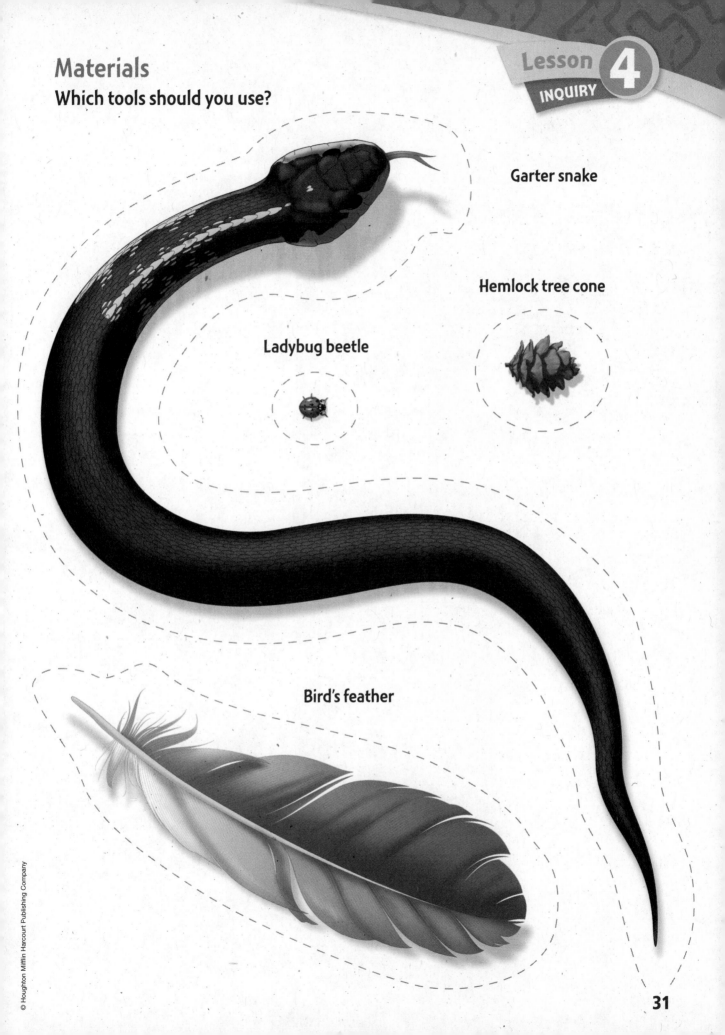

Materials
Which tools should you use?

Garter snake

Hemlock tree cone

Ladybug beetle

Bird's feather

Essential Question

How Do Scientists Use Data?

Engage Your Brain!

People sometimes make statues out of blocks. If you could count how many blocks of each color there are, how would you record this information?

_____

_____

_____

_____

Active Reading

Lesson Vocabulary

List each term. As you learn about each one, make notes in the Interactive Glossary.

_____   _____

_____   _____

_____   _____

_____

Main Ideas

The main idea of a section is the most important idea. The main idea may be stated in the first sentence, or it may be stated elsewhere. Active readers look for main ideas by asking themselves, What is this section mostly about?

Show Me the Evidence

Scientists use observations to answer their questions. You can do this, too!

Active Reading As you read these two pages, find and underline the definitions of *data* and *evidence*.

My data are my *evidence*. The data show that a raft with six planks floats twice as much weight as a raft with three planks.

Onisha, how do you know that a bigger raft can float more weight than a smaller one?

– I put the pennies on the raft with three planks. It held fewer pennies than the other raft.

Each science observation is a piece of **data.** For example, the number of pennies on a raft is data.

Onisha finished her investigation and thought about what it meant. She studied her data. Scientists use data as **evidence** to decide whether a hypothesis is or is not supported. Either way, scientists learn valuable things.

Scientists ask other scientists a lot of questions. They compare data. They repeat the investigation to see if they get the same results. Scientists review and talk about the evidence. They agree and disagree while respecting each other's ideas.

▶ Scientists might live too far away to meet face to face. What are three other ways they can share data and discuss evidence?

_____

_____

_____

_____

_____

_____

_____

Communicating Data

Scientists record and display data so others can understand it. There are many ways and many tools to do this.

How can I communicate my results?

Models can help us understand things that are too big, small, or dangerous to do or observe.

▶ You want to find how high different kinds of balls bounce. You test each ball 20 times. How will you record and display your measurements?

_____

_____

After you **gather data**, you can share, or **communicate**, it with others in different ways. How can you **record data**? To show how birds get seeds from a feeder, you can use a camera. If you observe how a dog cares for her puppies, write in a journal.

Sometimes scientists use charts and graphs to help **interpret** and **display data**. A **chart** is a display that organizes data into rows and columns. A **data table** is a kind of chart for recording numbers. A **bar graph** is used to compare data about different events or groups. Bar graphs make it easier to see patterns or relationships in data.

These students made a bar graph and a data table to compare results.

Maps, like this world map, help to show the relationships between different objects or ideas.

▶ You want to show kinds of weather in different places. How could you display this information?

_____

_____

▶ You want to show the different layers that make up Earth's crust. What could you use?

_____

_____

How To Do It!

What are some ways to display data? You can use data tables, bar graphs, and line graphs. How can students use displays to show what they observed in the butterfly garden?

Active Reading As you read these two pages, draw boxes around two clue words that signal a sequence, or order.

DATA TABLE

Month	Number of Butterflies
March	5
April	5
May	9
June	14

BAR GRAPH

Butterfly Garden

How do you create a graph? First, look at the data table. Each column has a heading telling what information is in that column. Now, look at the graphs. Did you notice that the same headings are used to name the parts of the graphs?

On the graphs, look at the line next to the heading "Number of Butterflies." It looks like a number line, starting at zero and getting larger. It shows the number of butterflies.

To complete the bar graph, find the name of a month along the bottom. Then, move your finger up until you reach the number of butterflies for that month. Draw a bar to that point. To complete the line graph, draw points to show the number of butterflies for each month. Then, connect the points.

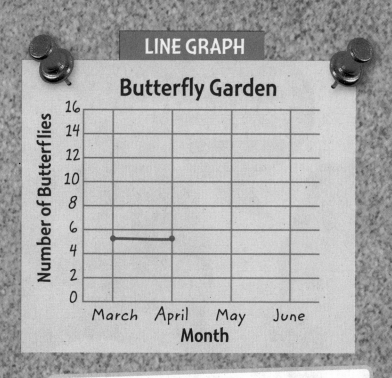

LINE GRAPH

▶ Now it's your turn. Use the data table to help you complete the graphs for the months of May and June.

Why Graphs?

Sharing information with others is important to scientists. How do graphs help us share?

I can share these results with other scientists. They can repeat the experiment to see if they get different results.

Why did you use a graph instead of a data table?

A graph helps you see information quickly and recognize patterns.

DATA TABLE

Class	Number of Cans
Room 5	40
Room 8	55
Room 11	20
Room 12	35
Room 15	45

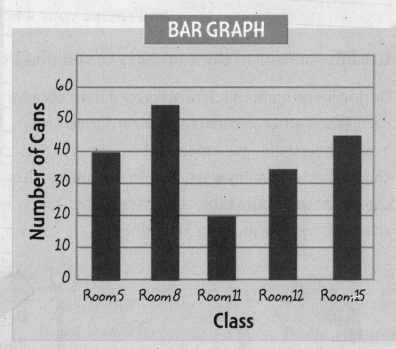

BAR GRAPH

Do the Math!
Interpret a Graph

Students collected evidence about a canned food drive in a data table. They organized the data in a graph.

1. Use the data table to find which class brought the least number of cans.

_____

2. Use the graph to find which class brought the greatest number of cans.

_____

3. Which was easier to use, the data table or the graph? Why?

_____

_____

_____

_____

_____

_____

When you're done, use the answer key to check and revise your work.

Use information in the summary to complete the graphic organizer.

During investigations scientists record their observations, or data. When other scientists ask, "How do you know?", they explain how their data supports their answers. Observations can be shared in many ways. Data in the form of numbers can be shown in data tables and bar graphs. Data can also be shared as models, maps, or in writing.

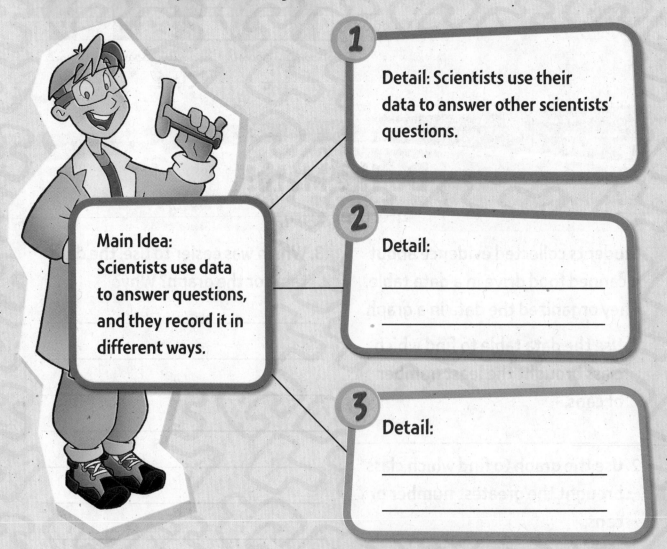

1

Detail: Scientists use their data to answer other scientists' questions.

Main Idea: Scientists use data to answer questions, and they record it in different ways.

2

Detail:
_____
_____

3

Detail:
_____
_____

Answer Key: 2. Data can be shown in data tables and bar graphs. 3. Data can also be shared as models, maps, or in writing.

Name _____

Word Play

Find the correct meaning and underline it.

1 Data
- tools used to measure
- steps in an investigation
- pieces of scientific information

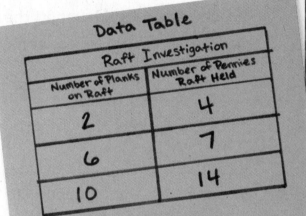

Data Table

Raft Investigation

Number of Planks on Raft	Number of Pennies Raft Held
2	4
6	7
10	14

2 Evidence
- a kind of graph
- how much space something takes up
- the facts that show if a hypothesis is correct

3 Data table
- a chart for recording numbers
- the number of planks on a raft
- a piece of furniture used by scientists

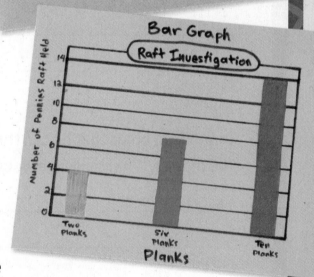

Bar Graph

Raft Investigation

4 Bar graph
- a chart for recording numbers
- a graph in the shape of a circle
- a graph that shows how things compare

5 Communicate
- take a photograph
- share data with others
- collect and record data

Apply Concepts

Read the paragraph and answer questions 6–7.

One morning, your dad walks you and your sister to the school bus stop. When you get there, you wonder, "Has the bus come yet?"

6 What evidence would support the idea that the bus has not arrived yet?

_____

_____

7 What evidence would support the idea that the bus had already come?

_____

_____

_____

8 Your friend brags that he can throw a baseball 100 meters. What evidence would prove this?

_____

_____

_____

Take It Home!

Share with your family what you have learned about recording evidence. With a family member, identify something you want to observe. Then decide how to record your data.

The Nature of Science Students gain scientific knowledge by observing the natural and constructed world, performing and evaluating investigations and communicating their findings. These principles should guide student work and be integrated into the curriculum along with the content standards on a daily basis.

Name _____

Essential Question

How Do Your Results Compare?

Set a Purpose
What will you learn from this investigation?

_____

_____

State Your Hypothesis
Tell how you think the height of bubbles in water relates to the amount of dishwashing liquid used.

_____

_____

_____

Think About the Procedure
List the things you did that were the same each time.

_____

_____

_____

Describe the variable, the one thing you changed each time.

_____

_____

_____

Record Data
In the space below, make a table to record your measurements.

Draw Conclusions

Look back at your hypothesis. Did your results support it? Explain your answer.

_____

_____

_____

_____

Analyze and Extend

1. Why is it helpful to compare results with others?

_____

_____

_____

2. What would you do if you found out that your results were very different from those of others?

_____

_____

_____

3. The bar graph below shows the height of the column of bubbles produced by equal amounts of three brands of dishwashing liquid. What does this data show?

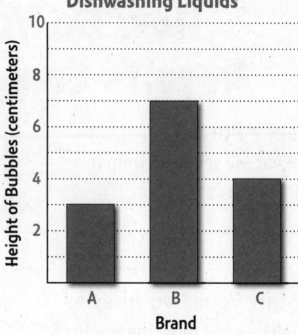

Bubbles Made by Dishwashing Liquids

_____

_____

_____

_____

4. Think of other questions you would like to ask about bubbles.

_____

_____

_____

_____

1

A meteorologist is a person who studies weather.

2

Meteorologists use tools to measure temperature, wind speed, and air pressure.

3

Meteorologists use data they collect to forecast the weather.

6

THINGS

You Should Know About

Meteorologists

4

Computers help meteorologists share weather data from around the world.

5

Keeping good records helps meteorologists see weather patterns.

6

Meteorologists' forecasts help people stay safe during bad weather.

Be a Meteorologist

Answer the questions below using the Weather Forecast bar graph.

1 What was the temperature on Thursday? _____

2 Which day was cloudy and rainy? _____

3 How much cooler was it on Tuesday than Thursday? _____

4 Which day was partly cloudy? _____

5 Compare the temperatures on Tuesday and Friday. Which day had the higher temperature? _____

6 In the forecast below, which day has the highest temperature _____? The lowest? _____

WEATHER FORECAST

Temperature °F

90

85

80

75

70

Monday   Tuesday   Wednesday   Thursday   Friday

Day of week

Multiple Choice

Identify the choice that best answers the question.

Nature of Science

1 Jamie does a simple experiment for homework. She needs to communicate the results. Which of these ideas is the BEST way to communicate her results?

- Ⓐ ask herself questions
- Ⓑ develop a conclusion
- Ⓒ form a hypothesis
- Ⓓ write a report

Nature of Science

2 A class is doing an experiment. The students want to know if tadpoles' health depends on the water they live in. They put tadpoles into two fish tanks. The table below shows what they did.

Tank	Water	Activity
A	clean tap water	Students will use treatments to clean the water.
B	clean tap water	Students will begin with clean water but will not keep it clean.

How is this science question being investigated?

- Ⓐ Students are classifying tadpoles.
- Ⓑ Students are researching.
- Ⓒ Students are experimenting using a variable.
- Ⓓ Students are building models.

Nature of Science

3 A student wants to find out if air takes up space. Which experiment would BEST help him find this out?

- Ⓐ Throw a paper airplane. Try it indoors and outdoors.
- Ⓑ Blow up a balloon and tie a knot. Try to flatten the balloon.
- Ⓒ Fly a kite on a windy day. See how high up the kite can go.
- Ⓓ Put red food coloring in an empty bottle, and cap it. Shake the bottle to see if the air inside turns red.

Nature of Science

4 Observe the shells shown below. What can you infer?

Shell 1   Shell 2   Shell 3

- Ⓐ They are all shells.
- Ⓑ Shell 1 has a rounded edge.
- Ⓒ Shell 2 had a skinny animal living in it.
- Ⓓ Shell 3 looks like a fan with a lot of lines on it.

Nature of Science

5 Four groups of students were told to measure the distance around a sandbox.

The results are shown below.

Group 1	80 cm
Group 2	798 cm
Group 3	800 cm
Group 4	798 cm

Compare the results. What should happen next?

Ⓐ Group 4 should change their results to 800 cm.

Ⓑ Group 2 and Group 4 should tell the class they are correct.

Ⓒ Group 1 should change their answer to match the other groups.

Ⓓ Group 1 should measure the sandbox again because their data is very different.

Nature of Science

6 While at the dog park, Noah notices only brown dogs and black dogs running around. Which statement below is a scientific observation?

Ⓐ There are no white dogs at the dog park today.

Ⓑ Brown dogs are healthy because they run around a lot.

Ⓒ Black dogs run faster than brown dogs because they eat more.

Ⓓ White dogs are probably not allowed at the dog park because they will get dirty.

Nature of Science

7 Sophie drew the parts of a plant. Then she described them to her class. How is Sophie doing an investigation?

Ⓐ She is inferring.

Ⓑ She is using a model.

Ⓒ She is gathering evidence.

Ⓓ She is making a hypothesis.

Nature of Science

8 Mr. Martinez's class is testing objects that sink or float. They will use computer models. Which might be a problem in using a computer model?

Ⓐ You can test materials that are not in your classroom.

Ⓑ You can test only what is in the computer program.

Ⓒ The class may not have a computer.

Ⓓ Not everyone will get to take a turn.

Nature of Science

9 Ava did an experiment with radishes. She concluded that radishes grow best in full sunlight. She presents her experiment at a science fair. Why should Ava include her data with her presentation?

Ⓐ so that the judges would have data to read

Ⓑ so that the judges would know she grew the plants

Ⓒ in case the judges would want to learn more about the topic

Ⓓ the judges could see if her data supported her conclusion

Nature of Science

10 Kia asks, "What types of trees grow the fastest?" She looks at this table.

Age of tree (years)	Height (meters)
1	2
5	3
10	4
20	6

Is there enough data for Kia to draw a conclusion?

Ⓐ Yes, in 20 years the trees grew to 6 meters tall.

Ⓑ Yes, you can compare the age of the tree with the height over time.

Ⓒ No, there is no data for the types of trees that grow the fastest.

Ⓓ No, there is no data for the age of the trees or the height they grew.

Nature of Science

11 Ilsa did an experiment to determine the height of bubbles that would form in jars with different amounts of soap. Her results showed that all the jars had the same height of bubbles. What conclusion can she make?

Ⓐ A different brand of soap would have made more bubbles.

Ⓑ More soap in the water means the height of bubbles would be greater.

Ⓒ The amount of this kind of soap does not affect the amount of bubbles.

Ⓓ Varying the amount of water in the jars would have made more bubbles.

Nature of Science

12 Frankie records the amount of rain that falls every day for a week. He wants to display his data to share the results. Which would be the BEST choice?

Ⓐ Make a bar graph.

Ⓑ Make a model.

Ⓒ Write a report.

Ⓓ Make a chart.

Nature of Science

13 Eduardo fills six jars with 400 milliliters of water. He places three of them outside in sunny spots and the other three in shady spots. He waits 4 hours and measures how much water is left.

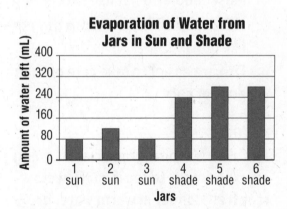

Evaporation of Water from Jars in Sun and Shade

Which conclusion is supported?

Ⓐ Water gets hotter in the shade.

Ⓑ Water gets hotter in the sun.

Ⓒ Water evaporates more quickly in the shade than in the sun.

Ⓓ Water evaporates more quickly in the sun than in the shade.

Nature of Science

14 The bar graph below shows the number of students who have different types of pets.

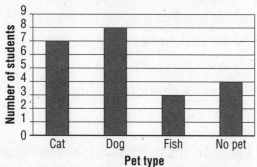

What Kind of Pet Do You Have?

Which statement is true and BEST supported by the data from the survey?

(A) Some students do not have pets.

(B) Most people do not like cats or dogs.

(C) Most people like cats more than they like dogs.

(D) Fish are easier to take care of than dogs or cats.

Nature of Science

15 Mrs. Harris's third-grade class is doing an experiment to see if cut flowers stay fresh longer in warm water or in cold water. Mrs. Harris created the table below.

	Roses	Daisies	Mums
Warm water			
Cold water			

What should students write in the different rows of the table?

(A) the length of each stem

(B) the size of each flower

(C) the date each flower wilts

(D) the number of petals on each flower

Nature of Science

16 Three students observed the outside air temperature throughout the day. Their data are shown below.

	Morning		Afternoon	
	8:15	**10:15**	**12:15**	**2:15**
Lucia	75 °F	78 °F	84 °F	89 °F
Josh	75 °F	78 °F	85 °F	88 °F
Emily	75 °F	77 °F	84 °F	88 °F

The students recorded temperatures from their own thermometers in the same area each time. What could be the BEST explanation for the slight differences in the temperatures they recorded?

(A) The students could not read the thermometers.

(B) The students looked at the thermometers at different times.

(C) One of the thermometers was broken, so its readings were different.

(D) Some readings were between the marks, so the students decided which mark was closest.

Nature of Science

17 Which is a science question about the natural world that can be tested in your back yard?

(A) How are airplanes designed?

(B) Which soil grows the most flowers?

(C) How fast can a race car travel?

(D) Which model of the planets is the best?

Nature of Science

18 The figure below shows two tools for measuring length.

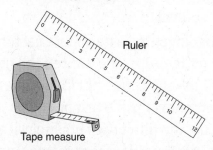

Ruler

Tape measure

Which item would be easier to measure using a 25-foot tape measure rather than a 12-in. ruler?

(A) a classroom

(B) a science book

(C) a postage stamp

(D) an insect, such as a beetle

Nature of Science

19 Mr. Cory's class measures the width of the classroom's doorway. Group A said the doorway is 1 m wide. Group B said the doorway is 100 cm wide. Mr. Cory says that both groups are correct. Why does Mr. Cory say that both groups are correct?

(A) A meter stick is shorter than a metric ruler.

(B) The metric ruler is more precise than the meter stick.

(C) The groups' measurements, 1 m and 100 cm, are the same length.

(D) When you use two different tools to measure the same object, you should get two very different answers.

Nature of Science

20 A class measures the outside air temperature at the same time each day for a month. Then they compare the data. Which tells the MOST precise information about the data?

(A) The coldest day was 5 °C.

(B) Many days were quite warm.

(C) It rained on several of the days.

(D) Some days were cooler than others.

Constructed Response

Nature of Science

21 Abigail works at an animal shelter where many kittens are born. She writes down the color of each kitten born during one week. She wants to show that half of all kittens born at the shelter were white that week.

Which would BEST show the information, a graph, table, or chart?

_____

Describe why your answer above would BEST show the information.

_____

Nature of Science

22 You have three magnets on your refrigerator. You want to know which one is the strongest magnet. What can you do to find out?

_____

How would you record your data?

_____

Nature of Science

23 The graph shows how bubbles form when liquid soap mixes with water of two different temperatures.

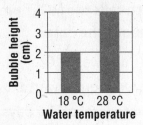

What does the graph above show?

_____

_____

What conclusion can you make based on the evidence?

_____

_____

_____

Extended Response

Nature of Science

24 Samuel's science group uses a pan balance to find the masses of three rocks.

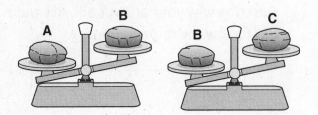

Write an observation about the masses of the rocks shown above.

_____

_____

Which rock has a GREATER mass, A or C? Explain the reasoning for your answer.

_____

Write an inference about rock A.

_____

Nature of Science

25 A scientist invented a new material for making coffee cups. She wanted the new material to keep coffee hot longer than the older foam cups. To test her new coffee cup, she fills it with boiling water. She also fills the older foam coffee cup with boiling water. The results of this experiment are shown below.

	Temperature	
Cup	**Start**	**After 1 hour**
new material	100 °C	85 °C
old foam	100 °C	85 °C

What tools did the scientist need for this experiment?

_____

What was the variable for this experiment?

_____

The scientist did this experiment 20 times, and the results were always the same. Why did the scientist do this?

_____

_____

Explain why the data shows that the scientist did not succeed.

_____

_____

_____

Sound and Light

STANDARD 1
Physical Science

University of Notre Dame
Marching Band

I Wonder Why

Why is the musician able to change the way the tuba sounds? *Turn the page to find out.*

Here's Why The tuba has valves the musician can press to make the notes higher or lower. He can change the force with which he blows into the mouthpiece to change the volume.

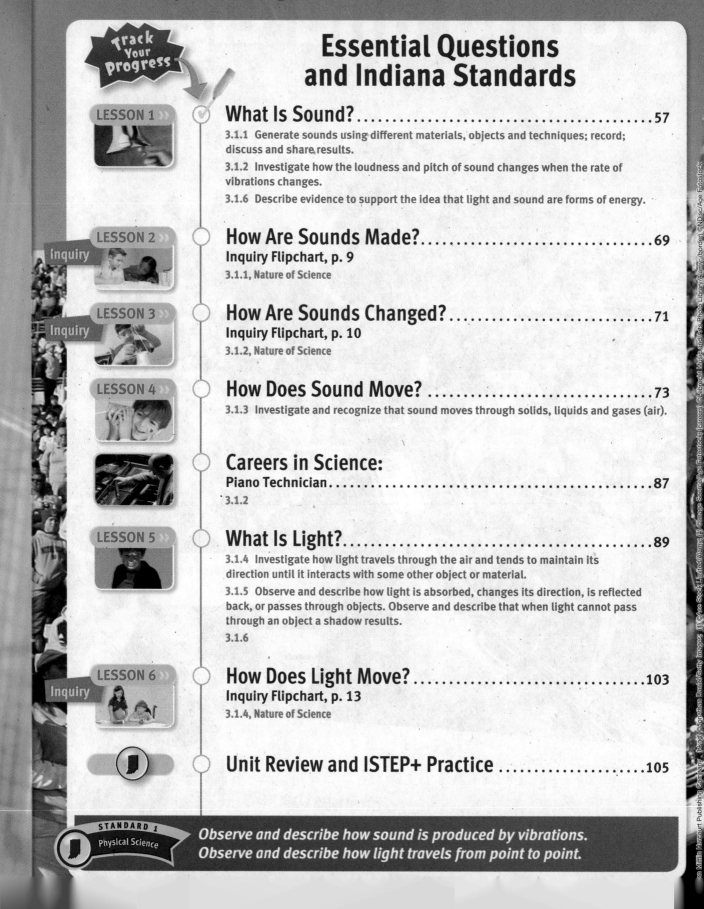

Track Your Progress

Essential Questions and Indiana Standards

STANDARD 1
Physical Science

Observe and describe how sound is produced by vibrations.
Observe and describe how light travels from point to point.

3.1.1 Generate sounds using different materials, objects and techniques; record; discuss and share results. **3.1.2** Investigate how the loudness and pitch of sound changes when the rate of vibrations changes. **3.1.6** Describe evidence to support the idea that light and sound are forms of energy.

Essential Question
What Is Sound?

Engage Your Brain!

Find the answer to the following question in this lesson and record it here.

Is a big drum louder than a small drum?

_____

_____

_____

Active Reading

Lesson Vocabulary
List the terms. As you learn about each, make notes in the Interactive Glossary.

_____

_____

_____

_____

Signal Words: Contrasts
Signal words show connections between ideas. Words that signal contrasts include *unlike, different from, but,* and *on the other hand.* Active readers remember what they read because they are alert to signal words that identify contrasts.

What Exactly Is Sound?

Sounds are all around us. Most of us hear sounds just about all the time. But how can you explain sound?

Active Reading As you read these two pages, draw a line under each main idea.

Let's start with a definition. **Energy** is the ability to make something move or change. An example of one form of energy is electricity. Think about ways electrical energy can make something move or change.

Sound is another form of energy. **Sound** is a form of energy that travels in waves. You'll read more about how sound travels later. In this lesson, you will learn about other properties of sound.

How can you tell that sound is energy? Maybe you've been in a thunderstorm that rattled the windows of your home. The thunder—sound energy—made the windows move.

Lightning is an example of electrical energy. It produces thunder, which is an example of sound energy. Lightning also produces heat and light— two more forms of energy.

Ordinary photographs are taken with light, which is a form of energy. But sound energy can be used to take pictures like this one of the inside of a cheetah.

© Houghton Mifflin Harcourt Publishing Company (bkg) ©Paul A Souders/Corbis; (t) ©AFP/Getty Images; (l) ©Dung Vo Trung/Politix/Corbis;

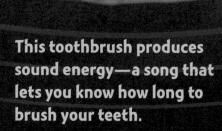

This toothbrush produces sound energy—a song that lets you know how long to brush your teeth.

Energy Sources

FORMS OF ENERGY

Type of Energy	Example
Sound energy	
Electrical energy	

What Makes Sound?

Now you know what sound is. But how is it produced?

Active Reading As you read these two pages, find and underline the definition of *vibrate*.

Sound is produced when something vibrates. **Vibrate** means "move quickly back and forth."

You can probably make your hand move quickly back and forth. Do you hear the sound it makes? Probably not. In order for something to make a sound that humans can hear, it has to move back and forth at least 20 times each second.

The jackhammer's motor vibrates, making noise. The tip of the jackhammer moves up and down very quickly. That makes more noise. Each time it moves down, it slams into the pavement, creating vibrations, and much more noise.

▶ In each picture, draw a circle around the thing or things that vibrate to make sound.

A housefly might beat its wings 200 times each second. That's what makes the sound you hear as the fly flies by.

The bell is designed to vibrate when the clapper hits it. That's why it rings. What if this person put the other hand on the bell? Then it wouldn't vibrate much. It wouldn't ring and it would just make a dull clunk.

When you strike a tuning fork, its arms vibrate. This one is designed to vibrate 440 times a second. That's why it makes a sound.

Up and Down

The guitar can play high notes and low notes, loud notes and soft notes. What makes these sounds different?

Active Reading As you read these two pages, draw boxes around the two clue words or phrases that signal one thing is being contrasted with another.

Do the Math!
Subtract

The A string on a guitar vibrates 110 times per second. The G string on a guitar vibrates 196 times per second. How many more times per second does the G string vibrate?

Pitch is how high or low a note or sound is. When something vibrates quickly, it makes a high-pitched sound. But when something vibrates slowly, it makes a low-pitched sound.

A housefly beats its wings 200 times each second. A mosquito beats its wings 1,000 times a second. Which one makes a higher-pitched sound when it flies?

loud noise

soft noise

Volume is how loud or soft a sound is. This guitar string was plucked with a lot of force. It is producing a loud sound.

This time the guitar string was plucked with less force. It is moving back and forth over a smaller distance. It is producing a softer sound.

Making Music Possible

What is the difference between music and sound? Music is a form of sound. But the musician controls the pitch, volume, and rhythm of the sound. If we couldn't change the pitch and volume of sound, there would be no music.

Only the part of the string below the musician's finger vibrates. The shorter the vibrating section is, the faster it vibrates. The faster it vibrates, the higher-pitched sound it makes.

The musician changes the volume by plucking the string harder or more softly.

The note is formed by air vibrating inside the tubes of the trombone. The movement of the slide controls the pitch of the note.

The musician changes volume by changing the force with which he blows into the mouthpiece.

Making Noise

Circle the parts of the instruments a musician uses to make sound.

Pressing the trumpet's valves changes the path of the air through the tubes. This can make the note higher or lower.

The musician changes volume by changing the force with which he blows into the mouthpiece.

Tightening the drumhead screws makes it vibrate more quickly. Tighter screws produce a higher note. Looser screws produce a lower note.

The musician changes the volume by hitting the drumhead harder or more softly.

Sum It Up!

When you're done, use the answer key to check and revise your work.

The idea web below summarizes the lesson. Complete the web.

Energy

1 Other forms of energy include electricity, light, and _____.

2 Sound is a form of _____.

3 Sound is produced when something _____.

4 The pitch of the sound depends on the _____ of the vibration.

5 The _____ of the sound depends on the force of the vibration.

Answer Key: 1. heat; 2. energy; 3. vibrates; 4. speed; 5. volume

Name _____

Word Play

1 Use the clues below to help you write the correct word in each row. Some boxes have been filled in for you.

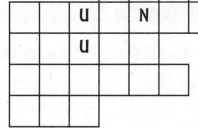

A.
B.
C.
D.
E.
F.
G.
H.

A. Move quickly back and forth.

B. How high or low a note is.

C. Something vibrating quickly makes this kind of sound.

D. Sound is a form of this.

E. Another word for volume.

F. Something that vibrates produces this.

G. The force of a vibration affects this.

H. A guitar string vibrating slowly produces this kind of note.

Apply Concepts

2 Circle the one that produces the fastest vibrations. Draw a square around the one that produces the slowest vibrations.

a bumble bee

a sousaphone

a dog barking

a saxophone

a mosquito

an airplane flying high overhead

3 When a string vibrates slowly, does it have a lower or higher sound? How about when a string vibrates quickly?

_____

_____

_____

4 How does a musician control sound to make music?

_____

_____

_____

Take It Home!

With your family, find three things in your home that make noise. Discuss the parts of each thing that vibrate to make the sound.

 3.1.1 Generate sounds using different materials, objects and techniques; record; discuss and share results. **Nature of Science**

Name _____

Essential Question

How Are Sounds Made?

Set a Purpose
What do you think you will learn from this experiment?

_____

_____

_____

_____

Think About the Procedure
How might you make one item produce a sound?

_____

_____

_____

_____

_____

_____

How might you make two items produce a sound?

_____

_____

_____

How might you change the sound that something produces?

_____

_____

Record Your Data
In the space below, make a table in which you record your observations.

Draw Conclusions

What can you conclude about the way items make sound?

_____

_____

_____

_____

Analyze and Extend

1. Pick an item you used to produce a sound, either by itself or with another item. Describe a real-life object that produces sound the same way.

_____

_____

_____

2. Describe something you did to change the sound that something produced. Then describe a real-life example of a sound being changed in the same way.

_____

_____

_____

3. Look around the classroom. Using what you have learned, what other items do you think you could use to make sound? Why?

_____

_____

_____

_____

_____

4. Think of other questions you would like to ask about how sounds are produced.

_____

_____

_____

_____

_____

3.1.2 Investigate how the loudness and pitch of sound changes when the rate of vibrations changes. **Nature of Science**

Name _____

Essential Question

How Are Sounds Changed?

Set a Purpose
What do you think you will learn from this experiment?

_____

_____

_____

State Your Hypothesis
Write your hypothesis, or testable statement.

_____

_____

Think About the Procedure
Why would you press your finger against the rubber band?

_____

_____

Why would you change the distance you pull the rubber band before you let it go?

_____

_____

_____

_____

Record Your Data
In the space below, make a table in which you record your observations.

Draw Conclusions

What can you conclude about how sound changes depending on how you pluck the rubber band?

_____

_____

_____

_____

Analyze and Extend

1. Did you make your observations with your eyes or with your ears? Why?

_____

_____

_____

2. How did the numbers on the ruler help you make accurate comparisons?

_____

_____

_____

3. How does the sound change depending on how hard or soft you pluck the rubber band?

_____

_____

_____

_____

4. Think of other questions you would like to ask about how sounds are produced.

_____

_____

_____

_____

Essential Question

How Does Sound Move?

Engage Your Brain!

Find the answer to the following question in this lesson and record it here.

If you were swimming underwater near this whale, would you be able to hear its song? Why or why not?

_____

_____

_____

Active Reading

Lesson Vocabulary

List the term. As you learn about it, make notes in the Interactive Glossary.

_____

Main Idea and Details

The main idea of a paragraph or section is the most important idea. The main idea may be stated in the first sentence, or it may be stated elsewhere. Active readers look for main ideas by asking themselves, What is this section mostly about?

What Is a Wave?

Sound is a form of energy that travels in waves. You may have seen waves on a lake or ocean. Do all waves move like that? Or are there different kinds of waves?

Active Reading As you read these two pages, underline the names of two different kinds of waves.

Water waves move up and down. You can see this if you look at a raft when a passing boat makes waves. When waves hit the raft, it bobs up and down.

In the ocean, waves move forward, but the water in the waves moves up and down. The two directions cross each other.

Sound waves move along the same direction a wave travels. Have you ever played with a spring toy? If you hold one end of the spring and move it forward and back, you make waves. What you see is a bunching up of some coils that moves down to the end of the spring and back. Spring-toy waves move along the spring.

▶ Draw a circle around each compressed section in the spring toy.

Look at the places where the coils are compressed, or bunched together. Each of them marks the start of a new wave.

Moving the rope up and down makes waves. The waves move along the rope from one end to the other.

Sounds and Gases

How will the alarm clock wake this girl? Sound waves will travel through the air to her ear.

Active Reading As you read these two pages, draw boxes around two clue words that signal a sequence or order.

The spring-toy wave moved in a straight line. But in the air, sound waves move outward in rings.

When a tuning fork vibrates, air particles move back and forth.

Air is a gas made up of tiny particles. Sound energy makes these particles move. That's why sound waves can travel through air.

Sound is produced when something vibrates. Imagine one arm of a vibrating tuning fork. First, it moves toward you and pushes the air particles in front of it. They bunch up. Then, it moves away from you. That leaves a space without many air particles. As this happens over and over, a pattern of bunched-up and spread-out air particles forms. This pattern is a sound wave.

▶ Draw Xs through each section of compressed air particles.

Sounds and Liquids

You have seen how sound waves travel through the air. But can they travel through other things, too?

Active Reading As you read these two pages, draw a line under each main idea.

Water is a liquid. Liquids are made up of tiny particles, too. Sound travels through liquids the same way it travels through gases.

Imagine a tuning fork vibrating under water. As it moves one way, water particles bunch up. As it moves the other way, they spread out. A sound wave moves through the water.

Sound travels through liquids about four times faster than it does through gases. The particles in liquids are packed more closely together than they are in gases. They do not have very far to go until they bump into the next particle. Because of this, sound waves move much faster. The speed of sound under water helps marine animals communicate over long distances.

Do the Math!
Adding Three Numbers

Sound travels through 20°C fresh water at about 1,500 m/sec. How far would a sound travel through this water in 3 seconds?

The dolphin is making a clicking sound. Sound waves are spreading out through the water just as they would through air.

Sound and Solids

Sound waves travel through gases. They travel through liquids. Can they travel through solids as well?

Active Reading As you read these two pages, draw boxes around the names of the two things that are being contrasted.

Sound waves travel through the string from one can to the other. If you could see these waves, they would look a lot like the waves in the spring toy.

Sound travels faster and farther through solids than it does through gases or liquids. This tracker can hear hoof beats through the ground before he can hear them through the air.

Like gases and liquids, solids are made of particles. The particles of gases and liquids move easily. The particles of solids don't move much. But they move enough to let sound waves through.

When vibrations strike a solid, they make the particles move just a little. The particles move back and forth. The sound wave travels through the solid.

▶ Draw an arrow on the string to show the direction in which sound waves are moving.

Hearing All the Sounds

You hear sounds that travel through the air. How often do you hear sounds that have traveled through liquids or solids? More often than you might think.

The sound of the lawnmower travels through the air (gas), the car window (solid), and more air (gas) before the girl can hear it.

The clouds are made up of drops of water, or liquid. The sound of the airplane travels through the air (gas), the cloud (liquid), the air (gas), the car window (solid), and the air (gas) before the girl can hear it.

▶ Complete the unfinished captions. Tell all of the things the sound travels through (and its state) before the girl hears the sound.

The sound of the dog barking travels through:

_____

_____

_____

_____

_____

before the girl can hear it.

The sounds of the children playing travel through:

_____

_____

_____

_____

_____

before the girl can hear them.

When you're done, use the answer key to check
and revise your work.

The blue part of each summary statement is incorrect. Rewrite each summary statement to make it correct.

1 The movement of water waves can be shown with a spring toy.

_____
_____

2 Sound travels faster through liquids than gases because the particles in liquids are spread far apart.

_____
_____

3 Air is made up of tiny bubbles that are too small to see.

_____
_____

4 When something vibrates, it makes the air particles around it move up and down.

_____
_____

5 Sound waves travel most quickly through liquids.

_____
_____

Answer Key: 1. sound waves 2. packed close together 3. tiny particles 4. bunch up and spread out 5. solids

Brain Check

Name _____

Word Play

1 Use the clues to help unscramble each word. Write the unscrambled word in the boxes.

A gas that is all around you.

R A I

☐☐☐ (first box circled)

Sound is produced when something

R I S A T V E B

☐☐☐☐☐☐☐ (first and sixth boxes circled)

Sound travels most quickly through this.

D O I L S

☐☐☐☐☐ (second and fourth boxes circled)

The kinds of waves you could show with a rope can also be see in this.

T R A W E

☐☐☐☐☐ (first box circled)

Ocean water is in this state.

Q U I L D I

☐☐☐☐☐☐ (fourth box circled)

Sound is a form of

E G R N E Y

☐☐☐☐☐☐ (second box circled)

Air is in this state.

S G A

☐☐☐ (third box circled)

Unscramble the letters in the circles to form a word that is related to this lesson.

_____

Apply Concepts

2 Circle the sound waves.

3 A clap of thunder sets your windows rattling. What actually presses against the window?

_____

_____

4 Describe a situation in which sound waves would travel through a gas, a liquid, and a solid on their way to your ear.

_____

_____

_____

_____

Take It Home!

With your family, look for objects that sound waves will travel through. Discuss whether the sound waves will travel through the objects quickly or slowly. Share your results with the class.

Ask a Piano Technician

Q. What is a piano technician?

A. A piano technician is a person who repairs and tunes pianos. When a piano is *in tune*, the notes it plays are all in the correct pitch.

Q. How do you tune a piano?

A. When you strike a piano key, a string vibrates and makes a sound. You change the pitch of the sound by tightening or loosening the string. A special tool is used to turn the pins that hold the strings. A tuning fork can give you the right pitch.

Q. What do you like best about your job?

A. I get to work in many different places. One day I might be tuning a piano in someone's home. The next day I might be fixing a concert hall piano.

Now It's Your Turn!

What question would you ask a piano technician?

_____

_____

_____

_____

Out of Tune!

1 How does a piano make sound?

_____

_____

_____

2 What does it mean when a piano is *in tune*?

_____

_____

_____

3 How do you change a sound's pitch?

_____

_____

_____

4 Why do piano technicians use tuning forks?

_____

_____

_____

3.1.4 Investigate how light travels through the air and tends to maintain its direction until it interacts with some other object or material: **3.1.5** Observe and describe how light is absorbed, changes its direction, is reflected back, or passes through objects. Observe and describe that when light cannot pass through an object a shadow results. **3.1.6** Describe evidence to support the idea that light and sound are forms of energy.

Essential Question

What Is Light?

🧠 Engage Your Brain!

Find the answer to the following question in this lesson and record it here.

What's wrong with the writing on the ambulance? It's backwards! Why?

_____

_____

_____

_____

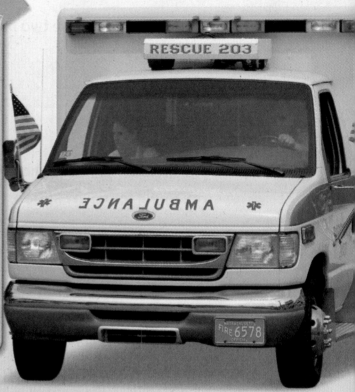

Active Reading

Lesson Vocabulary

List the terms. As you learn about each, make notes in the Interactive Glossary.

_____

_____

_____

_____

Cause and Effect

Signal words show connections between ideas. Words signaling a cause include *because* and *if.* Words signaling an effect include *so* and *thus.* Active readers remember what they read because they are alert to signal words that identify causes and effects.

Forms of Energy

Energy is all around us every day. It has many different forms.

Active Reading As you read these two pages, underline the names of forms of energy.

Examine Energy

How do you use energy in your home? Write an example for each caption.

Sound Energy

Sound comes from the speakers as music.

_____

_____

Electrical Energy

Electrical energy, or electricity [ee•lek•TRIS•ih•tee], is energy that moves through wires. It makes equipment work.

_____

_____

Heat Energy

Heat from the lights makes the musicians sweat.

_____

_____

Light Energy

Light from the spotlights helps the crowd see the band play.

_____

_____

A Lighted Path

Light is all around us. Light's movement allows us to see. How?

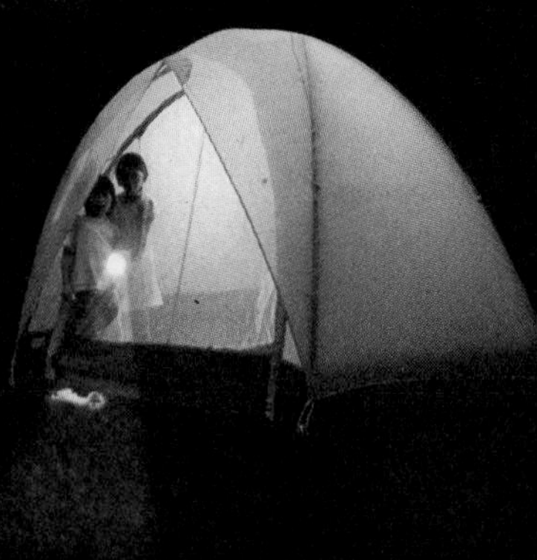

Active Reading As you read these two pages, draw a circle around the clue word that signals a cause.

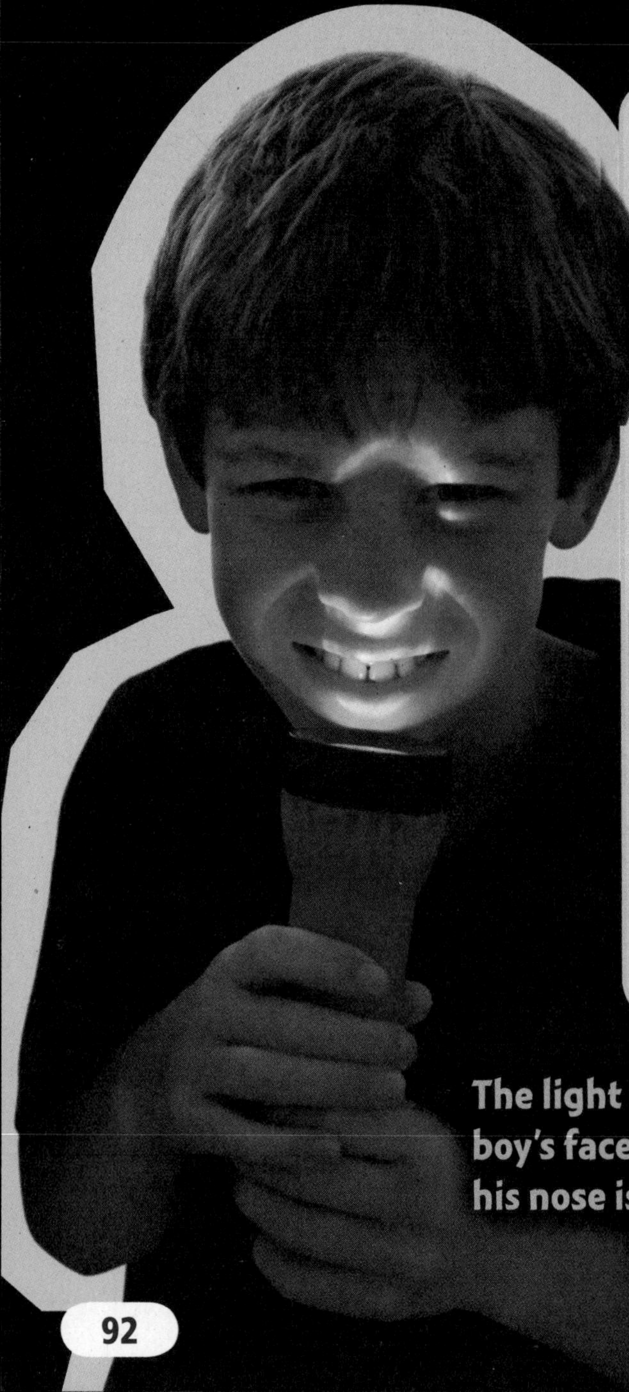

Light moves in straight lines. In the picture at the top of this page, the flashlight beam is a straight line. The beam does not bend or curve. Look at the picture below. The top of the light beam is a straight line, and the bottom of the light beam is a straight line. The whole light beam is straight.

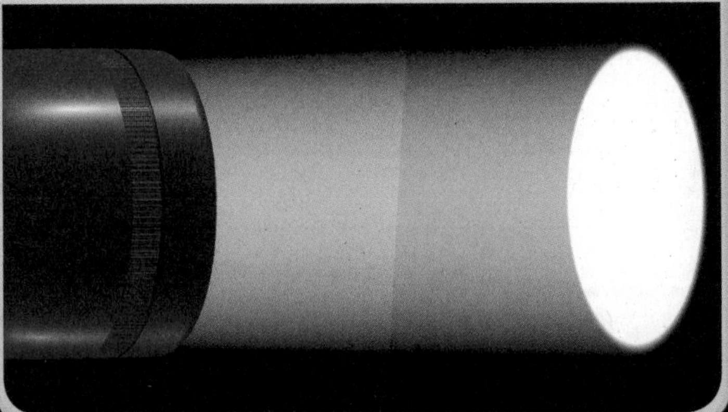

The light is below the boy's face. The shadow of his nose is above his nose.

What happens when light hits an object? It cannot keep going straight.

Objects can absorb light. **Absorb** means to take in. The marshmallow and the stick block light. They either absorb or bounce back all of the light that hits them. No light goes through.

The marshmallow and stick have a shadow. A **shadow** is the dark area behind an object that has blocked light. The shadow has a shape that is similar to the object. That's because light travels in straight lines.

The light in the tent is blocked by the kids' bodies. They absorb most of the light that hits them. You can see the shadows on the side of the tent.

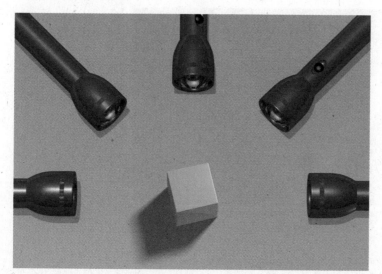

▶ One of these lights is on. It is making a shadow behind the block. Draw a circle around the light that is on.

Seeing Double

Not all objects absorb light. Some objects bounce light back in the opposite direction.

Active Reading As you read these two pages, find and underline three facts about reflecting.

A surface can **reflect**, or bounce back, light. Smooth glass, metal, and water reflect well. Picture a calm lake. The image on the lake is formed by light reflecting off its surface.

The beam of the flashlight below is shining downward. It traveled in a straight line until it hit an object that reflected it. The light bounced back up when it reflected.

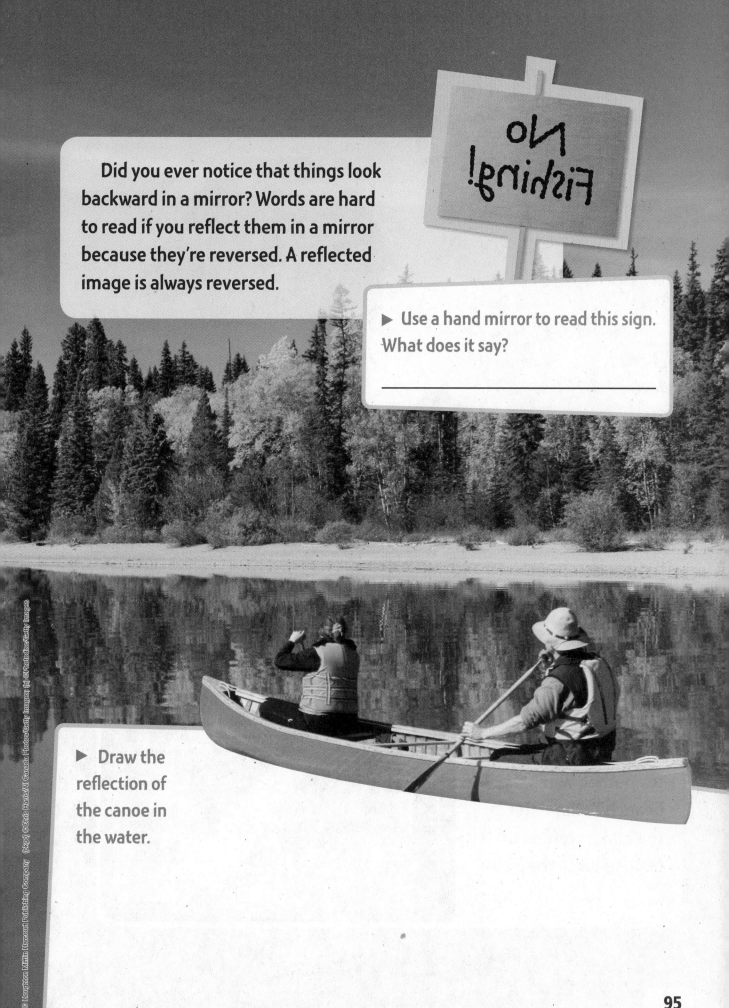

Did you ever notice that things look backward in a mirror? Words are hard to read if you reflect them in a mirror because they're reversed. A reflected image is always reversed.

▶ Use a hand mirror to read this sign. What does it say?

_____

▶ Draw the reflection of the canoe in the water.

Bend It!

Glass and water can reflect light. They can also bend light.

Active Reading As you read these two pages, underline the definition of *refract*.

refraction

Light can **refract**, or bend, when it moves from one clear material to another. When the beam hits the water in the tank, it refracts. It bends a bit to the right.

► Fill in the cause. Then circle the place in the photo where refraction occurs.

Cause

_____

_____

Effect

An object may appear broken

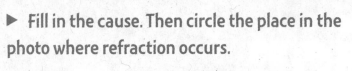

refraction

It's easy to see where light is refracted. Just look for the break! What makes the duck look broken? Light reflects from the duck above water and underwater. Light from the duck's top half goes straight to your eyes. Light from its bottom half goes through water first. The light refracts as it leaves the water. This makes the duck's belly and legs look separated from the top half of its body!

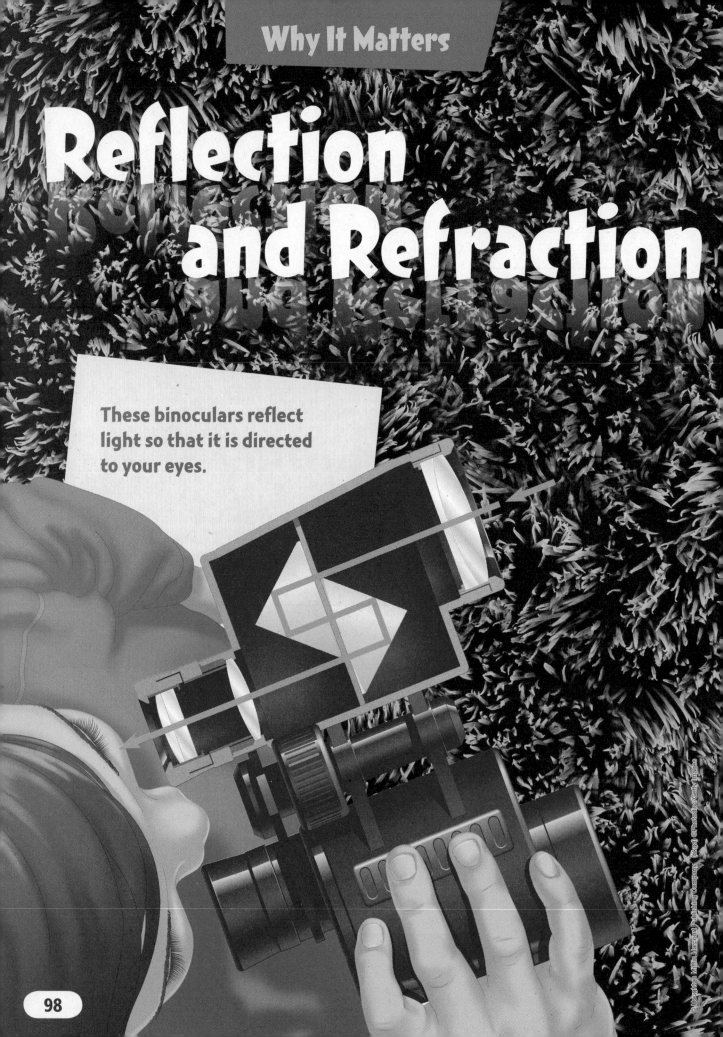

Reflection and Refraction

These binoculars reflect light so that it is directed to your eyes.

The lenses in this telescope refract light. This makes the object seem larger. Lenses in binoculars also refract light to make objects look larger.

If light didn't reflect, you'd never be able to see yourself in a mirror. If light didn't refract, there would be no telescopes, cameras, microscopes, or eyeglasses.

All of these items use lenses. Their lenses are made to refract. Items such as these depend on refracting lenses to work.

Do the Math!
Multiply Whole Numbers

Tom watches a robin. It appears about three inches in size. He then watches it through binoculars. The robin now appears to be nine inches in size. How many times as large did the robin look through the binoculars?

Sum It Up!

When you're done, use the answer key to check and revise your work.

Finish the summary statements. Then draw a line to match each statement with the correct image.

1 When light passes through a clear material, it bends, or _____ .

2 Some objects take in, or _____ light.

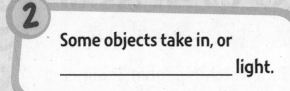

3 Behind an object that absorbs light, you will see a dark spot called a _____ .

4 When light hits a shiny surface, it bounces back, or _____ .

5 Light travels in a _____ path.

Answer Key: 1. refracts; connect to glass with straw. 2. absorbs; connect to rocks; 3. shadow; connect to boy with shadow. 4. reflects; connect to bowling pins and bowling ball. 5. straight; connect to flashlight

Brain Check

Name _____

Word Play

1 Use the words in the box to complete the puzzle.

How does light travel?

Down

1. Its purpose is to refract light.
2. An area that light cannot reach
3. To bounce back in the opposite direction
4. Bend, as light does when it moves from air to water
5. Marshmallows reflect and _____ light when it hits them.

Across

4. Objects in mirrors look like this
6. Uses lenses to reflect and refract light
7. The kind of path light travels in

absorb*   **binoculars**   **lens**   reflect*   refract*   **reversed**

shadow*   **straight**

* Key Lesson Vocabulary

Apply Concepts

2 Draw a circle around the item that reflects light. Draw a square around the item that refracts light. Draw a triangle around the item that absorbs light.

3 Label each diagram.

_____   _____

4 In the box, draw the path the light would take from the flashlight.

With your family, go through your home, looking for two things that reflect light, two things that refract light, and two things that absorb light.

Take It Home!

3.1.4 Investigate how light travels through the air and tends to maintain its direction until it interacts with some other object or material. **Nature of Science**

Name _____

Essential Question

How Does Light Move?

Set a Purpose
What do you think you will learn from this experiment?

_____

_____

_____

_____

State Your Hypothesis
Write your hypothesis, or testable statement.

_____

_____

_____

Think About the Procedure
What is changing during the activity?

_____

_____

How might you be able to determine the path of the light beam?

_____

_____

_____

Record Your Data
In the space below, make a table to record your observations.

Draw Conclusions

What can you conclude about the way light travels?

_____

_____

_____

_____

_____

Analyze and Extend

1. Does light always behave in the same way? How could you extend the inquiry to better answer that question?

_____

_____

_____

_____

2. Describe two real-life examples of light behaving the way it did during the inquiry.

_____

_____

_____

_____

_____

_____

_____

_____

3. Think of other questions you would like to ask about how light behaves.

_____

_____

_____

_____

_____

Multiple Choice

Identify the choice that best answers the question.

3.1.6

1 Marco's science class is studying different types of energy, such as electrical energy and sound. What is energy?

(A) Energy is the basic building block of all matter.

(B) Energy is anything that has mass and takes up space.

(C) Energy is the force that pulls all objects toward Earth.

(D) Energy is the ability to cause motion or change.

3.1.6

2 Which of the following is a form of energy?

(A) air

(B) light

(C) water

(D) Earth

3.1.1

3 When is sound produced?

(A) when something shines light

(B) when something vibrates

(C) when something is connected to a battery

(D) when something is pulled tightly

3.1.1

4 The picture below shows how Jacob is holding a rubber band.

What could you do to make a sound with Jacob's rubber band?

(A) blow on it

(B) make it longer

(C) make it shorter

(D) pull it and let go

3.1.2

5 Jan plucked the strings of a guitar. She noticed that each string produced a sound with a different pitch. What does pitch describe about a sound?

(A) how high or low the sound is

(B) how loud or soft the sound is

(C) how big the sound is

(D) how much energy the sound has

3.1.4

6 Rosa shined a flashlight down a hallway. The light could be seen along the hallway but not around the corner. Which of the following sentences BEST explains this?

(A) Light can be reflected.

(B) Light is a form of matter.

(C) Light travels in a straight line.

(D) Light travels in curved paths.

3.1.5

7 Lee is spending a day at the beach with his family. He decides to draw a picture of a nearby palm tree. The tree creates a shadow on the sand because it blocks light from the sun. Look at the shadow in Lee's picture below.

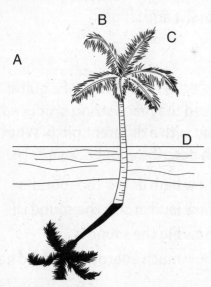

Where should the sun be in Lee's picture?

(A) position A

(B) position B

(C) position C

(D) position D

3.1.2

8 Sarah has a thick rubber band and a thin rubber band. If Sarah plucked each rubber band in the same way, how would the pitch of the thicker one compare with the pitch of the thinner one?

(A) The pitch of the thicker band would be higher.

(B) The pitch of the thicker band would be louder.

(C) The pitch of the thicker band would be lower.

(D) The pitch of the thicker band would be softer.

3.1.2

9 Max was experimenting with making sounds. He tapped his desk with a ruler and made a soft sound. What could Max do to make a louder sound with the ruler?

(A) tap the ruler against the desk using less force

(B) tap the ruler against the desk using more force

(C) gently swirl the ruler in a tub of water

(D) shake the ruler back and forth in the air with a lot of force

© Houghton Mifflin Harcourt Publishing Company (border) ©NDisc/Age Fotostock

3.1.5

10 The diagrams below show what can happen when light reaches an object. Which of the diagrams shows an object that reflects light?

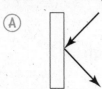

Ⓐ

Ⓑ

Ⓒ

Ⓓ

3.1.5

11 Beth was drinking a glass of water with a straw. She noticed that the straw appeared to bend as it entered the water as shown below.

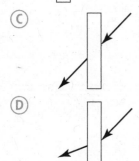

This is an example of which of the following?

Ⓐ absorption

Ⓑ reflection

Ⓒ refraction

Ⓓ transmission

3.1.4

12 Rylee and Ming hold opposite ends of a hollow tube that bends. They take turns shining a light through an end. They cannot see the light at the other end of the tube.

Why do you think that they cannot see the light?

Ⓐ The light that they are using is too dim, so it cannot travel that far.

Ⓑ Light travels in a straight line. The tube is bent, so the light cannot be seen.

Ⓒ The tube is too dark. If they try a tube of a lighter color, the light will show up.

Ⓓ The opening at both ends is not large enough to allow the light to enter and exit.

3.1.3

13 How does sound travel?

Ⓐ It travels in waves.

Ⓑ It travels as light rays.

Ⓒ It travels through space.

Ⓓ It travels in straight paths.

3.1.3

14 Which of the following statements BEST explains why you can hear a knock through a door?

Ⓐ Sound causes vibrations.

Ⓑ Sound moves at the speed of light.

Ⓒ Sound can travel through liquids.

Ⓓ Sound can travel through solids.

3.1.2

15 What happens to sound as the speed with which an object vibrates increases?

Ⓐ The sound gets higher.

Ⓑ The sound gets lower.

Ⓒ The sound gets louder.

Ⓓ The sound gets softer.

3.1.3

16 The table below shows the speed at which sound travels through different materials.

Material	Speed of Sound (m/s)
air	343
water	1,433
wood	3,300

What conclusion can you draw from these data?

Ⓐ Sound travels faster through air than through water.

Ⓑ Sound travels faster through wood than through water.

Ⓒ Sound travels faster through air than through wood.

Ⓓ Sound travels at the same speed through these materials.

3.1.5

17 Which of the following definitions BEST explains the term *reflect*?

Ⓐ to bend

Ⓑ to bounce back

Ⓒ to curve around

Ⓓ to go straight through

3.1.2

18 The picture below shows a rubber band stretched to two different lengths. The band can be plucked to make a sound.

Original length, 4 cm

A, stretched to 12 cm

B, stretched to 8 cm

What would you predict about the pitch of the sound of rubber band B compared with rubber band A?

Ⓐ The pitch of rubber band B would be higher.

Ⓑ The pitch of rubber band B would be louder.

Ⓒ The pitch of rubber band B would be lower.

Ⓓ The pitch of rubber band B would be softer.

3.1.4

19 A lighthouse produces a bright beam of light as shown below. The light travels in a straight line.

Which of the following would stop the beam of light?

Ⓐ The light reaches a mirror.
Ⓑ The light reaches a glass window.
Ⓒ The light reaches a waterfall.
Ⓓ The light reaches a rocky cliff.

3.1.5

20 Which of the following items would be MOST LIKELY to reflect light?

Ⓐ door
Ⓑ lamp
Ⓒ mirror
Ⓓ window

Constructed Response

3.1.5

21 Identify two ways that light can respond when it hits an object.

1. _____

2. _____

Make a diagram to show how light responds for each way you identified above.

1.

2.

3.1.2

22 You can make a sound with a straw by blowing through it. Describe what you could do to the straw to change the pitch of the sound it makes.

_____

_____

Describe what you could do to change the volume of the sound it makes.

_____

_____

_____

3.1.6

23 Compare light and sound. How are light and sound similar?

_____

_____

How do light and sound differ?

_____

_____

_____

Extended Response

3.1.5

24 Suppose you wanted to make shadows on a wall. What are two things you would need to make a shadow?

_____

_____

Make a diagram to show how these things need to be arranged in order to make a shadow. Include the wall and the two items you named above in your drawing.

What could you do to move the shadow toward the left on the wall?

_____

Why do shadows form?

_____

_____

3.1.1, 3.1.2

25 Stephanie and Lucas were doing an experiment to learn about sound. They recorded the pitch and volume of the sound a rubber band made when it was stretched or pulled in different ways. The table below shows their results.

Length (cm)	How we plucked the rubber band	Volume	Pitch
5	gently	soft	low
5	with a lot of force	loud	low
10	gently	soft	between low and high
10	with a lot of force	loud	between low and high
15	gently	soft	high
15	with a lot of force	loud	high

How do pitch and volume differ?

_____

_____

The rubber band was plucked in different ways. What effect did this have on the volume of the sound?

_____

_____

What effect did this have on the pitch of the sound?

_____

Using the data, describe the cause of the changes in pitch.

_____

_____

3.2.4 Observe fossils and describe how they provide evidence about the plants and animals that lived long ago and the nature of their environment at that time.

Essential Question

What Do Fossils Tell Us About the Past?

Engage Your Brain!

Find the answer to the following question in this lesson and record it here.

What can you learn about this dinosaur by studying its bones?

_____

_____

_____

Active Reading

Lesson Vocabulary

List the terms. As you learn about each, make notes in the Interactive Glossary.

_____

_____

Main Idea and Details

Detail sentences give information about a topic. The information may be examples, features, or facts. Active readers stay focused on the topic when they ask, What fact or information does this sentence add to the topic?

What Are Fossils?

Clues found in rocks tell us about plants and animals that lived long ago. What are some of these clues, and what can they tell us?

Active Reading As you read these two pages, draw a star next to what you think is the most important sentence.

Plants and animals that no longer live on Earth today are **extinct**. So how do we know about them? We can learn about extinct plants and animals that lived millions of years ago by studying fossils. A **fossil** is a trace or the remains of a plant or animal that died a long time ago.

Many fossils, like this ancient sea animal, are no bigger than your hand.

This fern lived millions of years ago. Today, ferns like this one are extinct.

Fossils give us clues about life long ago. The outline of a shell in rock may tell whether an area was once covered by water. A footprint fossil can give clues about the animals that lived in an area.

Fossil bones give clues about what an animal looked like, how big it was, or how it moved. A fossil tooth can show if an animal ate plants or other animals. Fossils might even tell if an animal cared for its young!

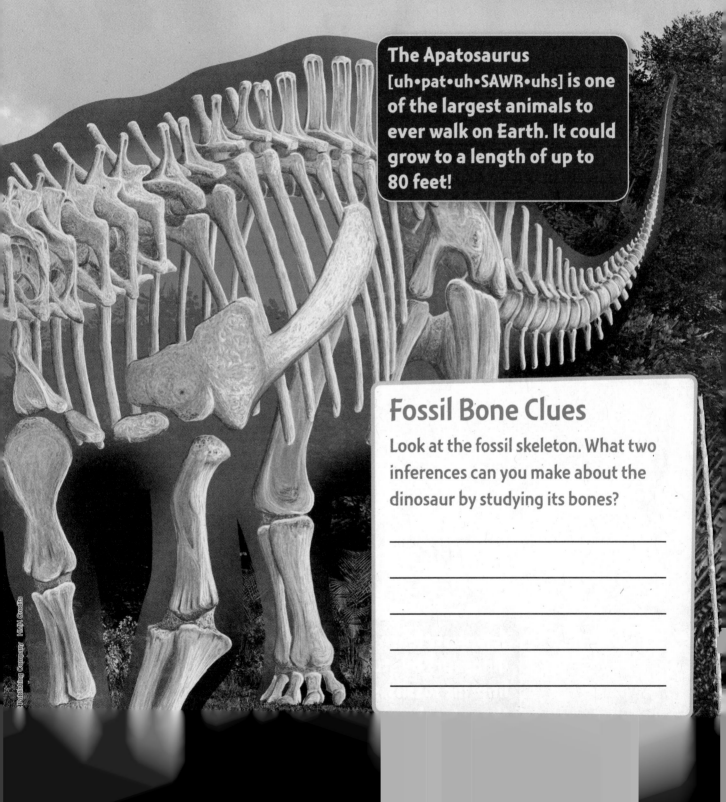

The Apatosaurus [uh•pat•uh•SAWR•uhs] is one of the largest animals to ever walk on Earth. It could grow to a length of up to 80 feet!

Fossil Bone Clues

Look at the fossil skeleton. What two inferences can you make about the dinosaur by studying its bones?

_____

_____

_____

_____

_____

Looking Into The Past

Leaves, branches, bones, and shells—most fossils form in rock. But they form in different ways. How do fossils form?

Active Reading As you read these two pages, draw triangles around the names of three kinds of fossils.

Look at the fossil footprints. They are *imprints*. An imprint forms when something presses into soil or mud. Later, the soil or mud changes to rock and becomes a fossil.

Scientists learn about dinosaurs by studying imprint fossils, such as these tracks.

Another kind of fossil is a *mold*. It is made when soil or mud covers the remains of an animal. The soft earth hardens into rock. Over time, water breaks down the remains of the animal in the rock. A hollow space is left in the shape of the animal. This hollow space is called a mold. If the space gets filled in with minerals, a *cast* forms. A cast fossil looks just like the animal that was covered by earth.

Dinosaur Tracks

Look at the imprint fossils. Write two inferences about the animal that made them.

_____

_____

_____

_____

This mold fossil formed over a long period of time.

This is a cast of a brachiopod. Most brachiopods are 1 to 2 inches long.

Fossils That Tell a Story

Fossils tell a story about life in the past. From fossils, we learn what Earth was like millions of years ago.

Fossils can tell us how Earth has changed over time. For example, suppose fossils of shells or other sea animals are found in places that are dry today. What can we learn? These fossils tell us that the environment was once covered by water. Fossils of plants found in an area can also tell us about the area long ago. Fossils of certain plants might suggest that a place was once very hot and wet.

The fossil beds at the Falls of the Ohio State Park in Indiana are clues that this area was once covered by an ocean of salt water.

Fossils tell us about the kinds of plants and animals of long ago. Some of them are now extinct. Others have changed very slowly over a long period of time. How do we know? We look to fossils for clues!

Do the Math!
Computation

At the Falls of the Ohio State Park, a scientist studies these fossils:

Fossil Type	Number
Imprint	87
Cast	152
Mold	176

How many more molds than casts does the scientist study?

_____

Sum It Up!

When you're done, use the answer key to check and revise your work.

The idea web below summarizes the lesson. Complete the web.

1

2

3

Kinds of Fossils

What Fossils Tell Us

4 Plants

5 Animals

6 Environment

Name _____

Word Play

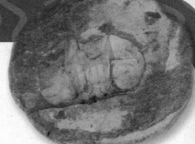

1 Unscramble letters to find each word. Use the hints to help you unscramble the letters.

1. D L O M

_____

Hint: a hollow space in rock in the shape of an animal

2. M I P N T R I

_____

Hint: animal tracks in rock

3. O S I F L S

_____

Hint: trace or remains of a plant or animal that lived a long time ago

4. T X I E T C N

_____

Hint: a plant or animal that no longer lives on Earth

5. S T A C

_____

Hint: a fossil in rock that forms inside a mold

Apply Concepts

2 Each of the pictures below shows a fossil. For each picture, write one observation and one inference that you can make from your observation.

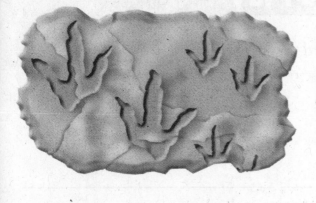 

_____   _____

_____   _____

_____   _____

_____

3 Choose one of the ways that fossils form and describe what happens. Draw a picture of a fossil that might form this way.

_____

_____

Take It Home!

Share what you have learned about fossils with your family. With a family member, use clay or dough to make an imprint fossil.

Essential Question

How Can We Use Natural Resources?

Engage Your Brain!

Find the answer to the following question in this lesson and record it here.

How do people use water to meet their needs?

_____

_____

_____

_____

Active Reading

Lesson Vocabulary

List the terms. As you learn about each, make notes in the Interactive Glossary.

_____

_____

_____

_____

Main Idea and Detail

Detail sentences give information about a topic. The information may be examples, features, or facts. Active readers stay focused on the topic when they ask, What fact or information does this sentence add to the topic?

Resources You Can Rely On

Many parts of Earth are covered by trees, water, rocks, and soil. All of the things people use come from these and other natural materials.

Active Reading As you read these two pages, draw two lines under each main idea.

Plants, water, air, and sunlight are just a few renewable resources we depend on to live.

Soil is a natural resource that people use to grow crops.

Life's Resources

In the photographs, circle the natural resources plants need to grow.

A **natural resource** is a material found in nature that is used by living things. Plants and animals use resources, such as air and water, to live. Plants use nutrients in soil and sunlight to grow. Animals use plants for food. People use soil to grow plants that are used for food or to make clothes. Air, water, nutrients, soil, sunlight, and plants are all natural resources.

Resources we use that can be replaced easily in a short time are called **renewable resources**. The water we drink is replaced by rain. Oxygen in air is replaced by plants. We replace trees and other plants by growing more of them. And we will never run out of sunlight!

141

nonrenewable Resources

Not all resources are replaced quickly. Some resources take thousands or millions of years to form.

Active Reading On this page and the next, circle phrases that show how nonrenewable resources are different from renewable resources.

Resources that aren't replaced easily are called **nonrenewable resources**. One example of a nonrenewable resource is fossil fuels. Coal, oil, and natural gas are fossil fuels. Some are used to produce electricity. Others run planes, cars, and other vehicles.

Because they form so slowly, there is a limited amount of fossil fuels and other nonrenewable resources. Once these resources are used up, they cannot be replaced. If people keep using fossil fuels at the same rate they do today, these fuels will be gone very soon.

Oil is found deep underground. It is pumped to the surface and then refined before it can be used.

Soil takes hundreds of years to form. It is made of weathered rock and once-living plants and animals.

Limestone and aluminum are mined. Limestone is used to make cement, and aluminum is used to make cans.

We all need to **conserve**, or save, fossil fuels. To conserve fossil fuels, you could turn off lights when you leave a room. What else could you do?

Other nonrenewable resources are rocks and minerals. Many rocks and minerals are mined. Once they are taken out of a mine, there are none left. It takes a long time for more rocks or minerals to form.

Another nonrenewable resource is soil. Soil can be washed away or polluted by trash or chemicals. Because of this, it is important for people to conserve soil.

Do the Math!
Interpret a Graph

The graph shows the percentage of different resources used to produce electricity in the U.S. How much comes from nonrenewable resources?

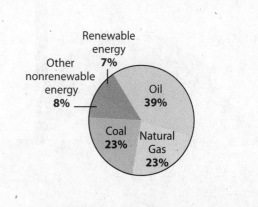

Renewable energy
7%

Other nonrenewable energy
8%

Oil
39%

Coal
23%

Natural Gas
23%

Resources for Every need

When you ride in a car, it uses a natural resource, such as fossil fuel. Paper, buildings, and heat for our homes also come from natural resources. For every need you can think of, some resource was used to meet it.

Oil is a fossil fuel. It is pumped from deep below ground using giant oil wells.

The oil is made into gasoline, or gas. Gas powers trucks, planes, and most cars. Some people use oil to heat their homes.

Rocks and minerals are natural resources used to build buildings, bridges, and tunnels. A quarry is a place where rocks are mined for use in building materials.

Lumber is made from the wood of trees. It is used to build houses and make paper products. Some clothing, such as cotton T-shirts and jeans, comes from plants, too.

Resources We Use

Circle the resources that are nonrenewable.

When you're done, use the answer key to check and revise your work.

Read the summary. Write each word from the list below in the correct box at the bottom of the page.

Everything people use comes from Earth's natural resources. Some of these resources are renewable. This means they can be replaced easily in a short amount of time. Many resources are nonrenewable. They cannot be replaced easily. In fact, some nonrenewable resources take millions of years to form.

rocks   sunlight

soil   trees and other plants

water   oil

natural gas   coal

minerals   air

1 **Renewable Resources**

2 **Nonrenewable Resources**

Name _____

Word Play

1 Look at each of the pictured natural resources in the first column. Then unscramble the letters in the second column to tell a way that people use the resource.

a.

A P E P R

☐ ☐ ☐ ☐ ☐

b.

L B G D I N U I

☐ ☐ ☐ ☐ ☐ ☐ ☐ ☐

c.

S L A O G N I E

☐ ☐ ☐ ☐ ☐ ☐ ☐ ☐

d.

E C E R I T L Y C T I

☐ ☐ ☐ ☐ ☐ ☐ ☐ ☐ ☐ ☐ ☐

Apply Concepts

2 Circle the renewable resource.

3 Circle the nonrenewable resource.

4 Think of two resources you read about. Write its name at the top of each box. Draw a picture of how people might use this resource. Tell if it is renewable or nonrenewable.

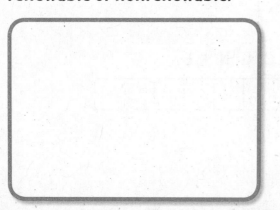 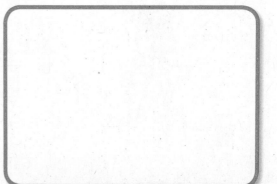

Take It Home!

With a family member, make a list of the natural resources you use in one day. Find out where each resource came from. Where does the cotton used to make a T-shirt come from?

148

Meet the Soil Scientists

Elvia Niebla

Elvia Niebla grew up in Arizona. Niebla studied hard in school and became a soil scientist. As a soil scientist, she helped seven states maintain their adobe buildings from the 1700s. Adobe is made of clay and sand. In 1984, Niebla started working for the government. She helped make rules to stop pollution in soil from getting into the food we eat. Now, Niebla studies how changes in the world's climate affect living things in our forests.

Pollution from industrial garbage can enter the soil on farms. People or animals can eat the plants that take in these poisons.

Brake ferns collect arsenic in their leaves. A measurement called pH can affect the amount of nutrients in soil. Scientists can test soil for the correct nutrients and pH.

Lena Qiying Ma

Lena Qiying Ma is a soil scientist at the University of Florida. She studies how plants take in arsenic [AR•suh•nik]. Arsenic is used as a poison to keep weeds away from crops. During her research, Ma found a fern growing in an industrial site. It was green even though the soil had arsenic pollution. Ma discovered that the fern removes arsenic from the soil. Ma studies how the fern can be used to clean up pollution in soil and ground water.

Be a Soil Scientist!

A farmer is planting his crops. He tests the pH of the soil from different fields on his farm. He wants to know what crop to plant in each field.

Use the pH scale to **match** the soil from each field with the best crop to plant in that field. Write the name of the crop on the line for the correct soil.

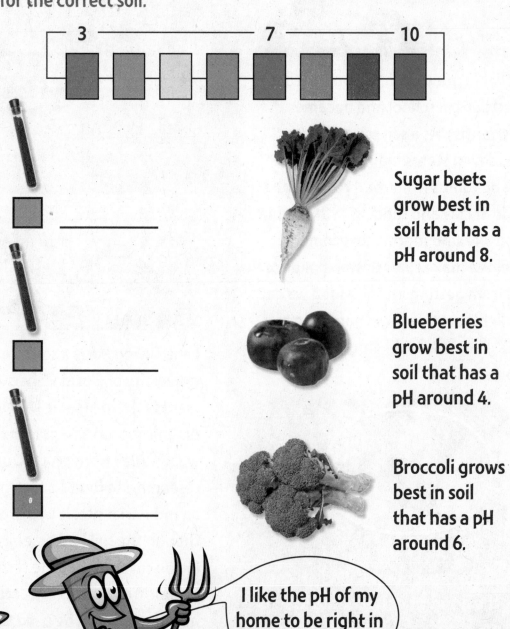

Sugar beets grow best in soil that has a pH around 8.

Blueberries grow best in soil that has a pH around 4.

Broccoli grows best in soil that has a pH around 6.

I like the pH of my home to be right in the middle!

Review and ISTEP+ Practice

Name _____

Multiple Choice

Identify the choice that best answers the question.

3.2.6

1 Many household items are made from renewable resources. Which of these objects is made from a renewable resource?

Plastic bag

Wooden spoon

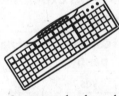

Computer keyboard

Oil

(A) Plastic bags are recycled, so they must be made from a renewable resource.

(B) Wooden spoons are made from the wood of trees, so they are made from a renewable resource.

(C) A computer keyboard is made from plastic, which is a mineral, so it is made from a renewable resource.

(D) Motor oil is made from petroleum that is formed deep underground, so this is a renewable resource.

3.2.2

2 Minerals can be formed in different ways. What is one way that minerals form?

(A) when rocks break apart

(B) when grass and plants decay and rot

(C) when magma cools and crystals form

(D) when scientists make them in a factory

3.2.2

3 A harder mineral can scratch a softer mineral. The Mohs hardness scale is shown below. On the Mohs scale, talc is the softest mineral, and diamond is the hardest mineral.

Mineral	Hardness
talc	1
gypsum	2
calcite	3
fluorite	4
apatite	5
feldspar	6
quartz	7
topaz	8
corundum	9
diamond	10

You have a mineral that scratches apatite but does not scratch quartz. What is the hardness of your mineral?

(A) greater than 2 and less than 4

(B) greater than 3 and less than 5

(C) greater than 4 and less than 6

(D) greater than 5 and less than 7

3.2.5

4 Jasmine is growing daisies in a window box outside her window. She makes sure that the daisies get all of the resources that they need. Which of the resources needed by the daisies is nonrenewable?

(A) Water is nonrenewable because it gets polluted.

(B) Sunlight is nonrenewable because it gets dark at night.

(C) Soil is nonrenewable because it takes millions of years to form.

(D) Air is nonrenewable because it is a resource that is not easily replaced.

3.2.6

5 Wind power is an energy source that causes very little pollution. Large modern windmills, called wind turbines, are turned by the wind to produce electricity. Which statement BEST explains why wind turbines are only used in some places to produce electricity?

(A) Wind power uses moving air that can be polluted.

(B) Wind power is nonrenewable, so it can only be used in some places.

(C) Wind is a renewable resource, but it is not windy everywhere.

(D) Wind power pollutes the air too much to be used everywhere.

3.2.2

6 Scientists can manufacture diamonds from carbon by using heat and pressure. These man-made diamonds are not classified as minerals. Which statement BEST explains why?

(A) They are made of glass.

(B) They are not naturally occurring.

(C) They do not have an orderly crystal structure.

(D) They are not the same color as real diamonds.

3.2.3

7 Tyrone was given a sample of four minerals. To test the hardness of each mineral, he tried to scratch each mineral with his fingernail, a copper penny, and a steel nail. The results of his experiment are shown in the table below.

Mineral	Fingernail	Copper penny	Steel nail
Calcite	no	yes	yes
Fluorite	no	no	yes
Gypsum	yes	yes	yes
Quartz	no	no	no

Which statement is correct?

(A) Gypsum is harder than calcite.

(B) Fluorite is harder than quartz and gypsum.

(C) Quartz is the hardest because nothing listed could scratch it.

(D) Gypsum is the hardest because everything listed could scratch it.

3.2.2

8 Minerals are identified and sorted by different characteristics. Luster is one way to sort minerals into different types. What is a mineral's luster?

(A) the way that light reflects from its surface

(B) the mineral's elements and their arrangement

(C) the color that it makes when rubbed on a tile

(D) the way that it breaks when you strike it with a wedge

3.2.3

9 Kenji's grandmother has a ring with a ruby in it. Kenji observes that the ruby has a luster similar to a window. Which word describes the luster of a ruby?

(A) The ruby has a greasy luster.

(B) The ruby has a glassy luster.

(C) The ruby has an earthy luster.

(D) The ruby has a metallic luster.

3.2.6

10 Limestone is a rock that is found under Earth's surface. It is a useful rock because it is used for building roads. Limestone is not found everywhere. Many of the old mines no longer have any limestone. What type of resource is limestone?

(A) Limestone is a new resource.

(B) Limestone is renewable resource.

(C) Limestone is a reservable resource.

(D) Limestone is a nonrenewable resource.

3.2.2

11 A tree is growing out of the rock shown below. What will MOST LIKELY happen to the rock after 50 years?

(A) The rock will melt and become a new rock.

(B) The rock will break apart and become smaller rocks.

(C) The rock will be washed away by ocean waves and become sand.

(D) The rock will be covered by lava, and heat will turn it into a different kind of rock.

3.2.2

12 Your teacher placed your class's rock collection into three groups. She said she classified them into groups called *sedimentary*, *igneous*, and *metamorphic*. Which BEST describes how she classified the rocks?

(A) She classified them by how they were formed.

(B) She classified them by their shape and size.

(C) She classified them by their luster.

(D) She classified them by their color.

3.2.6

13 A river flows over a dam, and a power plant uses the moving water to make electricity. What kind of resource is the moving water?

(A) renewable water energy

(B) renewable fossil fuel energy

(C) nonrenewable water energy

(D) nonrenewable sunlight energy

3.2.2

14 You are looking at a collection of rocks. What is MOST LIKELY true about these rocks?

(A) They have the same shape.

(B) They are made up of minerals.

(C) They have many fossils in them.

(D) They are made up of shells and sand.

3.2.1

15 Your teacher shows you a rock called sandstone. After you observe it, you notice that a tiny grain of sand fell off the rock. You wonder why that happened. What can you MOST LIKELY conclude based on your observation?

(A) Sandstone is not a rock.

(B) Sandstone breaks apart easily to form sand and soil.

(C) Sandstone falls apart easily because the grains are the color pink.

(D) Sandstone formed deep under Earth's crust and was once molten.

3.2.3

16 You are using a hand lens to look closely at table salt. Your teacher tells you that salt forms naturally. You notice that each piece is a tiny cube. Which statement BEST describes table salt?

(A) Salt is a substance made in factories.

(B) Salt is a mineral that has a crystal shape.

(C) Salt is a rock that is carved into cube shapes.

(D) Salt is a substance that forms crystals when water dissolves it.

3.2.3

17 You find a rock that is mostly made of feldspar and quartz. Use the table below to make an inference about the rock.

Mineral	Hardness
talc	1
gypsum	2
calcite	3
fluorite	4
apatite	5
feldspar	6
quartz	7
topaz	8
corundum	9
diamond	10

What is a reasonable inference you can make about this rock?

(A) It has talc in it.

(B) It is a soft rock.

(C) It has a hardness of 6.

(D) It has a hardness between 6 and 7.

3.2.4

18 Look at the drawing below showing rock layers. Rock layer 3 is a layer of rock with many ocean animal fossils in it. Rock layer 2 is formed of hardened lava. Rock layer 1 has many fern fossils in it. What can you infer about layer 2?

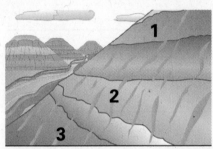

Ⓐ There were no animals alive when layer 2 was formed.

Ⓑ The area was a forest when the sediments were formed for layer 2.

Ⓒ There was too much weight from layer 1 above it for fossils to form.

Ⓓ There were no fossils in layer 2 because they were destroyed by lava.

3.2.4

19 The table lists some fossils found in one area. Which of the following is true?

Fossil	Age of Fossil
ocean shellfish fossils	600 million years old
insect fossils	300 million years old
dinosaur fossils	200 million years old
woolly mammoth fossils	5 million years old

Ⓐ Woolly mammoths died the most recently.

Ⓑ Shellfish are the youngest.

Ⓒ Dinosaurs lived before insects.

Ⓓ These fossils formed when the environment changed.

3.2.1

20 You are doing an investigation with rocks and soil. Your teacher gave you some rocks and a container with silt and sand mixed together. You need to sort everything from largest to smallest. You use a sieve to separate the silt and soil. Which shows your results from largest to smallest?

Ⓐ boulder, small rocks, sand, silt, pebbles

Ⓑ boulder, pebbles, small rocks, sand, silt

Ⓒ boulder, small rocks, pebbles, sand, silt

Ⓓ boulder, small rocks, pebbles, silt, sand

Constructed Response

3.2.5

21 Look at the picture below.

What plants do you see? What are two natural resources that plants need?

_____

_____

What animals do you see? What are two natural resources that animals need?

_____

3.2.3

22 You have three minerals, and you do not know what kind they are.

What are three things you can do to learn about the properties of each mineral?

_____

_____

_____

Using your fingernail, a copper penny, and a steel nail, how could you find out which of your minerals is the hardest?

_____

_____

3.2.5, 3.2.6

23 List two natural resources that people use and how they use them.

_____

_____

Explain why people need to conserve fossil fuels, such as gas and oil.

_____

_____

Extended Response

3.2.4

24 Press shells into clay to make a model of how fossils form. Fill the space made by the shell with plaster. After the plaster hardens, take it out of the clay. Think about the imprint of the shell compared to the plaster shape.

Which is the mold and which is the cast?

_____

How are these models like real fossils?

_____

How are these models different from real fossils?

_____

You find a tooth in the woods. Is it a fossil? Explain your answer.

_____

3.2.4

25 Look at the two fossils below.

dinosaur fossil   fern fossil

What kind of fossils are they?

_____

How were these fossils made?

_____

Write an observation and an inference about the first fossil.

_____

_____

Both of these living things lived about 40 million years ago. The fossils were found under glaciers in Canada. What can you infer about the environment of Canada 40 million years ago?

_____

_____

Plants

Pumpkins at a farm stand
in southern Indiana

PUMPKINS
$4⁰⁰
each

I Wonder Why

Some of these pumpkins are really big.
I wonder how they grew so large.

Turn the page to find out.

Here's Why The pumpkins started out as seeds. They grew into seedlings, then vines that formed pumpkins. With the right temperature and light, the vines and pumpkins grew larger and larger.

Track Your Progress

Essential Questions and Indiana Standards

STANDARD 3 Life Science

Observe, describe, and ask questions about plant growth and development.

Essential Question

What Are Some Plant Structures?

Engage Your Brain!

Find the answer to the following question in this lesson and record it here.

What do the roots at the bottom of this plant do for the plant?

_____

_____

Active Reading

Lesson Vocabulary

List the terms. As you learn about each one, make notes in the Interactive Glossary.

_____ _____

_____ _____

_____

Sequence

Many of the ideas in this lesson are connected by a sequence, or order, that describes the steps in a process. Active readers stay focused on sequence when they mark the transition from one step in a process to another.

Get to the Bottom of It

Plants come in many shapes and sizes. Did you know that an important part of most plants is hidden underground?

Active Reading As you read this page, circle lesson vocabulary words when they are defined.

Plants are made up of different parts. Each part has a function that helps the plant grow and survive.

The part of the carrot plant that we eat is its root. Roots hold plants in the ground. Roots also take in, or absorb [uhb•SOHRB], water and nutrients from the soil. **Nutrients** [NOO•tree•uhntz] are materials that living things such as plants need to grow.

Some roots are long and can reach water deep under the ground. Some roots have many small, hairy branches that spread out just under the soil to get water from a large area. Water and nutrients move from the roots to other parts of the plant.

A plant's roots absorb water and nutrients from the soil.

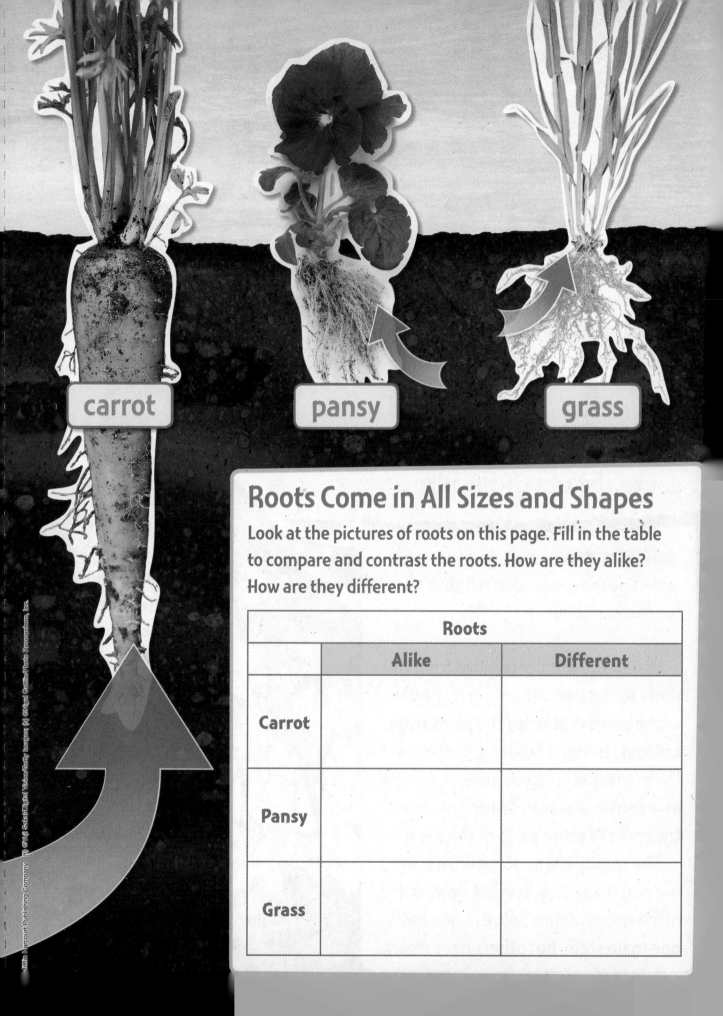

carrot

pansy

grass

Roots Come in All Sizes and Shapes

Look at the pictures of roots on this page. Fill in the table to compare and contrast the roots. How are they alike? How are they different?

	Roots	
	Alike	**Different**
Carrot		
Pansy		
Grass		

Reach for the Sky

What happens to water and nutrients after they enter the roots? How do they get to the rest of the plant?

A plant's stem carries water and nutrients from the roots to the rest of the plant.

Active Reading As you read this page, underline the details that tell about the functions of stems.

Water and nutrients move from the roots to the stem. The stem is the part of the plant that helps the plant stand tall and strong. It holds up the part of the plant that is above ground. A stem also carries water and nutrients from the roots to other parts of the plant.

The woody stems of most trees are big and thick. The stems of flowers are often soft and thin. Some plants have one main stem, but others have many.

passion vine

yellow daisy

Do the Math!
Make a Graph

Use the data to create a bar graph to compare the lengths of different plant stems.

Type of Plant	Length of Stem
Dogwood tree	650 cm
Bamboo	400 cm
Broccoli	50 cm
Saw palmetto	200 cm

Plant Stem Length

Length of Stem (cm)

700
600
500
400
300
200
100
0

Dogwood Tree   Bamboo   Broccoli   Saw Palmetto

Type of Plant

Plant Food!

Water and nutrients keep a plant healthy. But a plant still needs food to survive. Luckily, a plant doesn't need to go anywhere to get its food!

Active Reading As you read these pages, draw one line under a cause. Draw two lines under an effect.

Unlike animals, most plants can make their own food. This important process takes place in leaves.

Leaves use water, air, and light energy from the sun to make food. The food is then transported from the leaves through the plant's stems to other parts of the plant. Plants use most of this food energy to live and grow. The rest of the food is stored.

sunflower

Leaves use water, air, and sunlight to make food. Food made in leaves is transported to the rest of the plant.

palm tree

Leaves are many different sizes and shapes. Look at the picture of the sunflower plant. Its leaves are big and wide. Big, wide leaves can catch more sunlight. This helps the plant make more food.

bush

Show the Flow

Draw a plant growing in soil. Draw different-colored arrows to show how water, nutrients, and food move in different directions through the plant.

The Cycle of Life

The tallest tree in the world was once small enough to fit in your hand. Like you, plants start out small and grow bigger.

Active Reading As you read this page, write numbers next to the appropriate sentences to show the order of steps in the reproduction of an apple tree.

The blossoms on apple trees and other plants are called flowers. A **flower** is the plant part that helps some plants reproduce [ree•pruh•DOOS]. When living things **reproduce**, they make new living things like themselves.

First, flowers grow into fruit. After the fruit ripens, it falls to the ground. The fruit contains seeds. A **seed** has a small plant inside of it. A seed also has food for the small plant.

Then sunlight, soil, water, and air help the seeds sprout into seedlings and grow. The seedlings grow into adult plants. The life cycle continues as the adult plants produce more flowers and seeds.

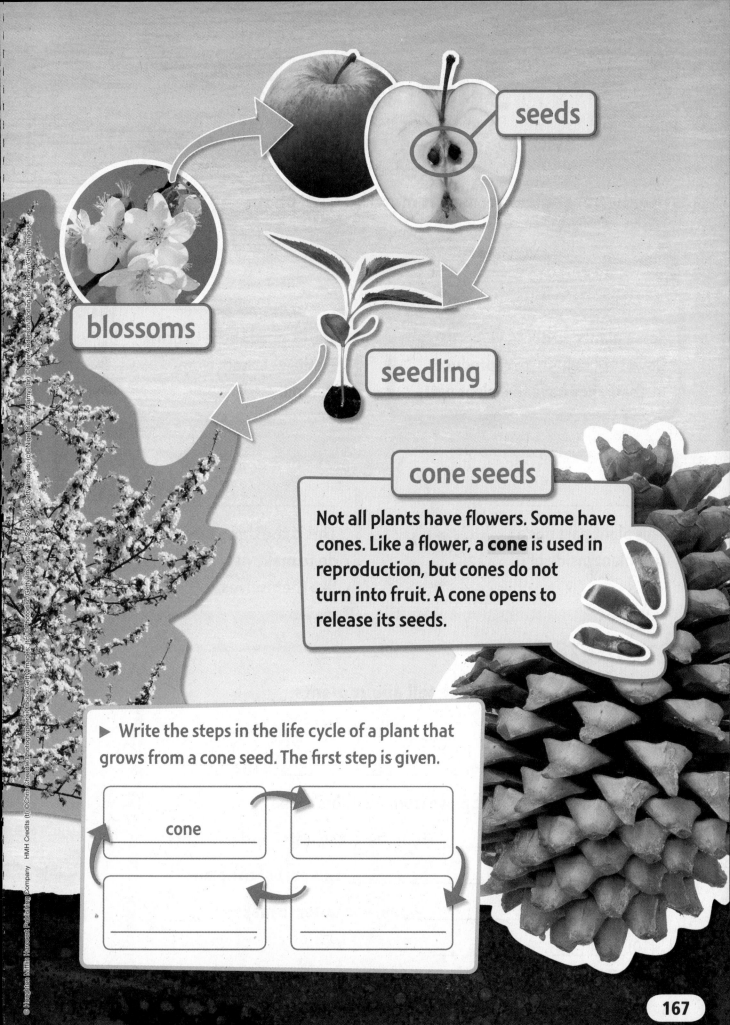

seeds

blossoms

seedling

cone seeds

Not all plants have flowers. Some have cones. Like a flower, a **cone** is used in reproduction, but cones do not turn into fruit. A cone opens to release its seeds.

▶ Write the steps in the life cycle of a plant that grows from a cone seed. The first step is given.

cone

Sum It Up!

Write the vocabulary term that matches each photo and caption.

1 _____

Some plants do not have flowers to help them reproduce. Instead, they have this plant part.

2 _____

Plants need these to grow. Plants get them from the soil.

3 _____

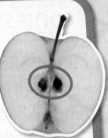

This plant part has a tiny plant inside of it.

4 _____

This is the thing plants do to make new plants like themselves.

Summarize

Fill in the missing words to tell about plants.

The (5) _____ of the plant absorb water

and nutrients from the (6) _____. The

water and nutrients next move from the roots to the

(7) _____. From there, the water and nutrients

move to the (8) _____. This part of the plant

uses (9) _____, air, and water to make

(10) _____.

Name _____

Word Play

1 Use the words in the box to identify the parts of a plant. Tell one function of each part.

| roots | stem | leaf | flower* | *Key Lesson Vocabulary |

_____
_____
_____

_____
_____
_____

_____
_____
_____

_____
_____
_____

Apply Concepts

2 Draw the life cycle of a peach tree. The first stage is already done.

Find two different types of plants near your school.

3 How are these plants different?

_____

4 How are these plants similar?

_____

5 Which parts of the two plants can you see?

_____

Take It Home!

Work with a family member to grow a plant you can eat. When the plant is fully grown, discuss its different parts and how they help the plant. Then share it with your family as a snack!

5 Things to Know About Rosa Ortiz

1
Rosa Ortiz is a botanist. She studies plants.

2
Ortiz studies a family of plants called the moonseed family.

3
Moonseed is a woody vine. It has poisonous parts.

4
Ortiz travels to many places to study moonseed.

5
The roots of some types of moonseed have been used as medicine.

Now You Be a Botanist!

1 What do botanists study?

2 How can studying plants help people?

3 Which part of the moonseed has been used as medicine?

4 Draw a picture of a woody vine. Label the stem, leaves, and root.

1 _____
_____
_____

2 _____
_____
_____

3 _____
_____
_____

4

3.3.1 Observe and identify the common structures of a plant including roots, stems, leaves, flowers, fruits, and seeds, and describe their functions. **3.3.2** Investigate plant growth over time, take measurements in SI units, record the data and display them in graphs. Examine factors that might influence plant growth. **Nature of Science**

Name _____

Essential Question

How Do Plants Grow?

Set a Purpose

In this investigation, you will observe plant seeds several times. Why do you think scientists make multiple observations?

_____

_____

_____

_____

_____

Think About the Procedure

Predict what will happen to the seeds.

_____

_____

_____

_____

_____

How can you make sure you are measuring accurately?

_____

_____

_____

_____

_____

_____

Record Your Data

In the space below, make a graph to show how the plant grew over time.

Draw Conclusions

What did you observe? Infer why the
seeds responded this way.

_____

_____

_____

_____

_____

_____

Analyze and Extend

1. Compare your observations with
   those of other groups. Did all
   groups have the same results?
   Why or why not?

_____

_____

_____

_____

_____

2. Your seeds have grown for 10 days.
   What do you think will happen to
   them in another 10 days if you do
   not water them?

_____

_____

_____

_____

_____

_____

_____

3. Think of other questions you
   would like to ask about the way
   seeds grow.

_____

_____

_____

_____

_____

3.3.1 Observe and identify the common structures of a plant including roots, stems, leaves, flowers, fruits, and seeds, and describe their functions. **3.3.2** Investigate plant growth over time, take measurements in SI units, record the data and display them in graphs. Examine factors that might influence plant growth.

Lesson **3**

Essential Question

How Do Plants Respond to Their Environment?

Engage Your Brain!

Find the answer to the following question in this lesson and record it here.

This tree fell over and then began growing upward again. Why?

_____

_____

_____

Active Reading

Lesson Vocabulary

List the terms. As you learn about each one, makes notes in the Interactive Glossary.

_____

_____

Main Idea and Details

Detail sentences give information about a topic. The information may be examples, features, characteristics, or facts. Active readers stay focused on the topic when they ask, What fact or information does this sentence add to the topic?

Plants and Light

What happens when you go from a dark room into a bright room? You blink! Blinking is a response to light. Plants respond to light, too.

Active Reading As you read these two pages, draw two lines under each main idea.

Hi. My name is Maria. I like learning about plants. One day, I put my plant in a dark room with one window. A week later, it looked like this! The plant began growing toward the light.

Growing toward light is one way that plants respond to their environment. The **environment** is all the living and nonliving things in a place. Growing toward light helps plants make more food.

Morning glory flowers open in the morning sun and last only one day.

By afternoon, the flowers close up and die.

Flowering plants respond to light in more than one way. The flowers of some plants open during the day and close at night. Other plants have flowers that open at night and close during the day. The bright yellow flowers of the sunflower plant face the sun throughout the day. The flowers move from east to west, following the sun as it crosses the sky.

What Will the Plant Do?

Look at the picture of the plant on the opposite page. Imagine that you turned the plant around so that it was growing away from the light. Explain and draw what would happen to the plant.

_____

_____

Hot or Cold?

What happens when it's very warm outside? You sweat! Sweating is a response to heat. Plants respond to heat, too. What happens when it's really cold outside? Your teeth chatter! Plants also respond to cold weather.

In winter, the apple tree was bare. In spring, the temperature got warmer. The apple tree was covered with buds. Temperature can also help seeds germinate (JER•muh•nayt). **Germinate** means that the seeds of the plant start to grow. Apple seeds must go through several weeks of near freezing temperatures before they will germinate.

This tree grows buds in the spring.

If the temperature gets too cold, this apple will be ruined.

However, weather below 0°C, or a *freeze*, can harm a plant. Sometimes the freeze happens when the plant is flowering. The flowers are damaged, and the plant will not produce fruit. Sometimes the freeze happens when the fruit is on the tree. The fruit is damaged!

Some plants need cold temperatures. Hyacinth bulbs must have cooler weather before they will grow again in the spring.

Do the Math!
Interpret a Graph

The graph shows the number of ripe apples picked from Maria's tree for five years. Study the graph, and then answer the questions.

Number of Apples on Maria's Tree

Year	Apples
2006	🍎🍎🍎🍎🍎🍎🍎
2007	🍎🍎🍎🍎🍎🍎
2008	🍎🍎
2009	🍎🍎🍎🍎🍎🍎🍎🍎
2010	🍎🍎🍎🍎🍎🍎🍎🍎🍎🍎

Key: Each 🍎 = 2 boxes

1. How many apples were picked each year?

_____

_____

_____

_____

2. In which year do you think a freeze occurred? Why?

_____

_____

_____

Up or Down?

What happens when you jump? Gravity pulls you back. Plants respond to gravity, too.

Active Reading As you read this page, find and underline details about a plant responding to gravity.

Gravity pulls things toward Earth's center. A plant's roots respond to gravity by growing mostly downward. A plant's stem responds in the opposite way. The stem grows upward, away from the pull of gravity. Even when a plant gets tipped on its side, the plant's stem will slowly start to grow upward again.

Stems grow up.

Roots grow down.

Growing against the pull of gravity gave this tree a bend in its trunk.

I know that gravity makes plant roots grow downward and stems grow upward. So what would happen if I turned a bean plant on its side?

1

The stem of this bean plant grows upward, away from gravity.

2

On its side, the bean plant's stem continues to grow opposite the pull of gravity.

▶ Predict what the plant will do if the pot is turned upright again.

_____

_____

_____

3

▶ Draw what the plant will look like after a few weeks.

Sum It Up!

When you're done, use the answer key to check and revise your work.

Complete the graphic organizer using details from the summary below.

Plants respond to their environment. They grow toward light. Plant leaves bud and seeds germinate when the temperature is right. Their roots and stems grow in certain directions in response to the pull of gravity.

1 Detail: _____

Main Idea: Plants respond to their environment.

2 Detail: _____

3 Detail: _____

Answer Key: 1. Plants grow toward light. 2. Plant leaves bud and seeds germinate when the temperature is right. 3. Plant roots and stems grow in certain directions in response to gravity.

Name _____

Word Play

1 Use the words and the clues in the box to complete the puzzle.

Across

2. This determines when some seeds grow
4. Forming flowers or leaves

Down

1. This pulls things toward Earth's center
3. All the living and nonliving things around a living thing
5. Begin to grow

budding   environment*   germinate*   gravity   temperature

*Key Lesson Vocabulary

Apply Concepts

2 Add an arrow from the cause to the effect.

3 In the image above, what is tree doing in response to the heat?

_____

4 Draw arrows to show which direction roots and stems will grow in response to gravity.

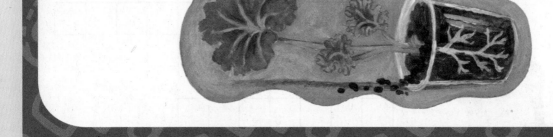

5 What is happening in the picture?

_____

_____

_____

_____

Take It Home!

Share what you have learned about plant responses with your family. Explain how a plant responds to light, temperature, and gravity.

3.3.1 Observe and identify the common structures of a plant including roots, stems, leaves, flowers, fruits, and seeds, and describe their functions. **3.3.2** Investigate plant growth over time, take measurements in SI units, record the data and display them in graphs. Examine factors that might influence plant growth. **Nature of Science**

Name _____

Essential Question

How Do Plants Respond to Light?

Set a Purpose
Write a researchable question to guide your investigation.

_____

_____

_____

_____

_____

Think About the Procedure
Why were all the holes the same size?

_____

_____

_____

_____

_____

Predict what will happen to the seedlings.

_____

_____

_____

_____

Record Your Data
In the space below, draw how the seedlings responded to light.

Draw Conclusions

What did you observe? Infer why the
seedlings responded as they did.

_____

_____

_____

_____

_____

Analyze and Extend

1. Compare your observations with
   those of other groups. Did all
   groups have the same results?
   Why or why not?

_____

_____

_____

_____

_____

2. Plants respond to temperature as
   well as light. How could you design
   an experiment to find out how
   temperature affects plants?

_____

_____

_____

_____

_____

_____

_____

3. Think of other questions you
   would like to ask about the way
   plants grow.

_____

_____

_____

_____

_____

Multiple Choice

Identify the choice that best answers the question.

3.3.1

1 Martin puts a seedling plant in a glass of blue water. He knows the flower will absorb the water. In what order will the water travel through the parts of the plant?

- Ⓐ leaves, roots, stem
- Ⓑ roots, leaves, stem
- Ⓒ roots, stem, leaves
- Ⓓ stem, leaves, roots

3.3.1

2 Look at the diagram of a plant below. Which part of the plant absorbs water from the soil?

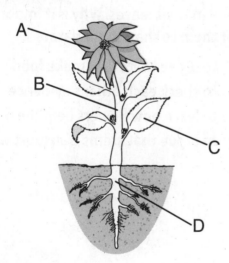

- Ⓐ flower
- Ⓑ stem
- Ⓒ leaves
- Ⓓ roots

3.3.1

3 Katrina observes the plant part shown below with a hand lens. Which statement BEST describes what Katrina can write in her notebook about this plant part?

- Ⓐ It is the part that gets water from the ground.
- Ⓑ It is the part of the plant in which food is made.
- Ⓒ It is the part of the plant that will bloom into a flower.
- Ⓓ It contains a small plant that can grow into a larger plant.

3.3.1

4 Jamal notices the needle-like leaves on an evergreen tree in his yard. Which one of the following BEST describes what the needles do for the plant?

- Ⓐ support the plant
- Ⓑ make food for the plant
- Ⓒ transport water to the roots
- Ⓓ produce seeds for the plant to reproduce

5 Carlos has drawn the picture below of a plant. He labels one part of the plant and marks it A.

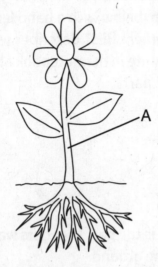

What caption should Carlos write next to the letter A?

Ⓐ makes food

Ⓑ absorbs water

Ⓒ anchors the plant

Ⓓ carries nutrients

3.3.1

6 Erin wants to prove that a stem transports water from the roots to other parts of the plant. Which of the following would BEST demonstrate this function?

Ⓐ Place a plant in the dark.

Ⓑ Put foil over the leaves of the plant.

Ⓒ Place a white carnation in blue water.

Ⓓ Add nutrients to the soil of a potted plant.

3.3.1

7 Layla knows that people can eat certain plant parts. Which of these is a root that people eat?

Ⓐ an apple

Ⓑ a carrot

Ⓒ a pine cone

Ⓓ broccoli

3.3.1

8 Dante is studying the plant part in which food is made. Which plant part is Dante studying?

Ⓐ the plant's leaves

Ⓑ the taproot

Ⓒ seeds from inside the fruit

Ⓓ the plant's stem

3.3.1, Nature of Science

9 Rex's data tell him that plant roots store food. Lily's data tell her that plants make food in their leaves. Why is it important for them to share their data?

Ⓐ to prove that roots make food

Ⓑ to check each other's evidence

Ⓒ to learn how flowers help the plant

Ⓓ to prove that stems transport water

3.3.2, Nature of Science

10 Izzy and Becca grew bean seedlings and measured the length of each plant's stem.

Day	Bean 1	Bean 2
1	1	0.5
2	1.5	1
3	2	2.5
4	3	5
5	5	6

What is the most important thing they forgot to include in their chart?

Ⓐ measurements of the roots
Ⓑ which day they started
Ⓒ the unit of measurement
Ⓓ who measured which bean

3.3.2, Nature of Science

11 Gabe measured the root length as a seed sprouted. His data showed there was no growth between Days 4 and 5, but Gabe is sure the root grew. What is the most likely explanation?

Ⓐ By Day 4, the root grew as long as it could grow.
Ⓑ No one watered the plant on Day 4.
Ⓒ He used a different ruler on Day 5.
Ⓓ He forgot to measure on Day 4.

3.3.2

12 Plants respond to light. The leaves of a plant use light to make food. In what other way do plants respond to light?

Ⓐ Their stems grow shorter.
Ⓑ Their roots grow deeper.
Ⓒ Their leaves become smaller.
Ⓓ Their flowers open and close.

3.3.2

13 Gravity, light, and temperature are three parts of a plant's environment. The table below shows how plants respond to these parts of their environment.

Plant Responses

Gravity	Light	Temperature
?	stems grow toward light	some pine cones open

Which of the following choices goes in the blank space in the table?

Ⓐ buds open
Ⓑ seeds sprout
Ⓒ flowers blossom
Ⓓ roots grow downward

3.3.2

14 Sari noticed that the roots on the seeds she planted grow down into the soil. Which statement best describes the seeds' response to the environment?

Ⓐ The seed is responding to gravity.
Ⓑ The cold keeps roots from coming out of the ground.
Ⓒ Sunlight is making the roots grow downward.
Ⓓ Warm temperatures make the roots grow downward.

3.3.2

15 How might freezing temperatures affect orange tree flowers?

Ⓐ The flowers die.
Ⓑ The flowers germinate.
Ⓒ The flowers grow upward.
Ⓓ The flowers turn into fruit.

3.3.2, Nature of Science

16 Jan's experiment shows that plants grow toward light. She wants to show others what she observed. How can she best record her results?

(A) Draw a picture.

(B) Make a bar graph.

(C) Write a paragraph.

(D) Make a data table.

3.3.2, Nature of Science

17 You have just finished an experiment about plants and light. After one week, your results showed that plants grow toward light. Your classmate's results showed that plants do not grow toward light. How could you best solve this problem?

(A) Change your results so that they match.

(B) Conclude that the experiments were a complete waste of time.

(C) Examine the records to find out why the results differ.

(D) Stand firmly behind your results because plants always grow toward light.

3.3.2

18 All plants respond to their environment. How do plants respond to temperature?

(A) The right temperature can make buds bloom.

(B) The right temperature can make pine cones close.

(C) The right temperature can make leaves grow smaller.

(D) The right temperature can make flowers grow down.

Nature of Science

19 What is one of the main reasons that scientists share their findings?

(A) to remember what they discovered

(B) to prove that they were working in the lab

(C) so other scientists can use their work to make additional discoveries

(D) so other scientists will be careful not to make any mistakes

3.3.2, Nature of Science

20 Prashant set up an experiment to see how his plant would respond to light. What would be the best prediction of what will happen after one week?

(A) The plant will change color.

(B) The flower will close.

(C) The plant will grow toward the light.

(D) The roots will dry up.

Constructed Response

3.3.2, Nature of Science

21 Liz is walking along a wide trail in the woods. She notices that there are some small trees along the path that are in the shade of some large trees. The branches of the smaller trees are growing sideways over the path. The branches of the larger trees are growing in a much more upward direction.

What part of the environment are the branches responding to?

_____

_____

Explain why the trees have these differences.

_____

_____

_____

_____

_____

3.3.1, 3.3.2, Nature of Science

22 Lois places a bean seed and a wet paper towel in a cup. What can she predict will happen? Explain why.

_____

_____

_____

_____

_____

_____

_____

3.3.2

23 Compare how roots and stems respond to their environment.

_____

_____

_____

_____

_____

_____

Extended Response

3.3.1

24 Study the plant diagram below.

For each letter in the diagram, write the name of the part the line is pointing to. Then write at least one function of each plant part.

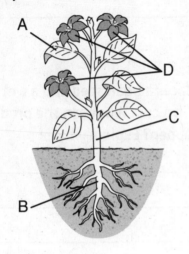

A _____

_____

_____

B _____

_____

_____

C _____

_____

_____

D _____

_____

_____

3.3.2, Nature of Science

25 Your class is designing an experiment to investigate how plants respond to temperature. You are given three similar plants for the experiment.

Describe how you will set up the experiment for the three plants.

_____

_____

_____

What other materials will you need for the experiment?

_____

_____

_____

How will you use the materials to make sure that only one variable is tested?

_____

_____

_____

Describe the observations and measurements you will make for the experiment.

_____

_____

_____

Measuring and Simple Machines

STANDARD 4
Science, Engineering and Technology

PROCESS STANDARDS
Design Process

Union Station in Indianapolis, Indiana

I Wonder How

This building was built in 1853. How has the building process changed since then? Stayed the same? *Turn the page to find out!*

Here's How Today, builders use more complex and electric tools than they did in 1853. But they still have to draw plans, choose materials, and make sure the building is safe to use.

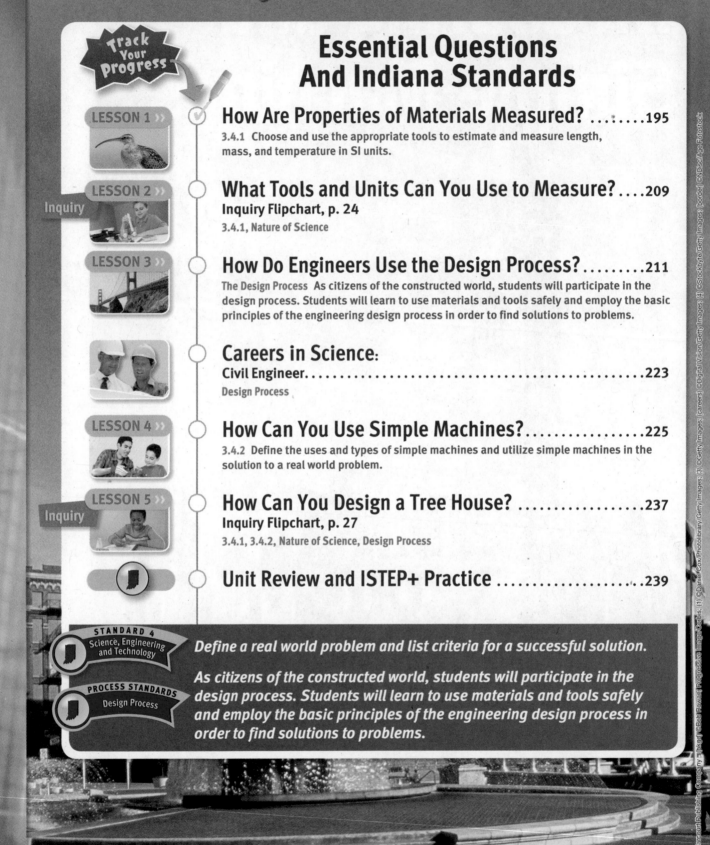

Track Your Progress

Essential Questions And Indiana Standards

STANDARD 4
Science, Engineering and Technology

Define a real world problem and list criteria for a successful solution.

PROCESS STANDARDS
Design Process

As citizens of the constructed world, students will participate in the design process. Students will learn to use materials and tools safely and employ the basic principles of the engineering design process in order to find solutions to problems.

3.4.1 Choose and use the appropriate tools to estimate and measure length, mass and temperature in SI units.

Lesson 1

Essential Question

How are Properties of Materials Measured?

Engage Your Brain!

Can you identify these objects?
How can you describe them?

_____

_____

_____

_____

Active Reading

Lesson Vocabulary

List each term. As you learn about each one, make notes in the Interactive Glossary.

_____   _____

_____   _____

_____   _____

Compare and Contrast

Ideas in parts of this lesson explain comparisons and contrasts, or how things are alike and different. Active readers focus on comparisons and contrasts when they ask questions such as, How are these things alike? How are they different?

It's Everything!

These snowmen are very different from the people building them. Yet the snowmen and the people are also alike. How do you think they are alike? How are they different?

Active Reading As you read these two pages, underline the names of the things that are being compared.

Each snowman is matter. It is made of three round, white snowballs. One snowball is big, one is medium-sized, and the other is small. What physical properties can describe the people building it?

The snowmen and the people are both made of matter. **Matter** is anything that has weight and takes up space.

Scientists use physical properties to describe matter. A **physical property** is something that tells us about matter. You already use many physical properties to describe objects. Color is one physical property. Shape is another physical property that tells about matter.

These skis are matter. They are hard. One set is longer than the other. What other physical properties do they have?

▶ How is the snow on ground different from the snow used to build the snowmen? How are they alike?

_____

_____

_____

The Long and the Short

This girl is holding a pole bean and a green bean. The pole bean gets its name from one of its physical properties. Can you guess which one is the pole bean?

Active Reading As you read these two pages, underline the clue words that signal lengths are being compared.

The pole bean is about as long as the girl's forearm. The green bean is shorter, or about the length of her finger.

Another physical property that describes matter is length. **Length** is a measurement of distance between two points. Compare the length of the pole bean to the girl's forearm. Most third-graders have forearms that are about 21 centimeters long. Can you *estimate,* or make an educated guess, of the length of the bean in centimeters?

This curlew has a long, hooked bill to probe into the mud and find small, crab-like animals.

Scientists use tools to take exact measurements. A ruler or tape measure lets scientists measure the exact length of an object. A metric ruler uses units called centimeters. Between each centimeter are lines for even smaller measurements called millimeters. **Millimeters** are tenths of a centimeter.

Look at the two birds on this page. One has a shorter bill. The other has a longer, curved bill. You could use a metric ruler to compare the lengths of the two beaks.

This stone-curlew's short bill helps it dig up insects in the sand.

Mass

All matter takes up space and has mass.

Active Reading Find the sentence that tells the meaning of mass. Draw a line under the sentence.

Another physical property that describes matter is mass. **Mass** is the amount of matter an object has. A bowling ball has more mass than a table-tennis ball. There is more matter that makes it up. Scientists measure mass using units called **grams**.

A soccer ball weighs more than a tennis ball because it has more mass. It needs to be bigger so there is more space to kick it.

table-tennis ball
_____

golf ball
_____

tennis ball
_____

baseball
_____

Mass is also a measure of how hard it is to move an object. The more mass an object has, the harder the object is to move.

Look at the balls on this page. Which do you think is the heaviest? Do you think it is easier or harder to move than the lightest ball?

▶ Use the table that shows the mass of each ball in grams and write the correct mass next to each ball.

Type of Ball	Mass
Table-Tennis Ball	3 g
Golf Ball	46 g
Tennis Ball	58 g
Baseball	145 g
Football	410 g
Soccer Ball	426 g
Bowling Ball	6,350 g

The light weight of a baseball makes it easy to throw and catch.

bowling ball
_____

soccer ball
_____

football
_____

Measuring Mass

There is something you can use to measure mass. It is called a pan balance. So, how does it work?

Active Reading As you read these two pages, number the steps in measuring mass.

A tool called a **pan balance** is used to compare masses. The pine cones in the picture below make the pan balance tilt to the left. That tells you pine cones have mass. But it doesn't tell you how much mass. To measure the mass, you must balance them with objects with a known mass.

A pan balance is like a seesaw. It will tilt down under the more massive object.

To measure the mass of the pine cones, place a gram mass on the opposite pan. Add gram masses one at a time until the balance does not tilt to one side or the other.

Each of the gram masses is marked with how much mass it has. When the pans on both sides balance, the masses on both pans are equal. Add up the numbers on the gram masses. This is the mass of the pine cones.

Your Turn!

Draw a picture of what would happen if a large dog and small dog sat down on opposite ends of a seesaw.

Do the Math!
Measure

What is the mass of the pine cones in each example?

1. To measure the mass of one pine cone, Celia used three 1-gram masses.

   _____

2. Josh measured the mass of four large pine cones. He placed one 10-gram, one 5-gram, and two 1-gram masses on the opposite pan.

   _____

3. Christine and Chloe measured the mass of seven pine cones. They used two 10-gram masses and two 1-gram masses.

   _____

Hot and Cold

At the lake, you might do different things depending on if it is hot or cold. One way you can tell if the weather is hot or cold is by knowing the temperature.

Active Reading As you read the next page, underline the sentence that explains what a thermometer does.

The children are swimming in the lake, so that means the water must be warm!

Solids, liquids, and gases have temperatures. **Temperature** tells us how hot or cold matter is. It is not scientific to describe an object as "hot" or "cold." Scientists need exact measurements. A **thermometer** is a scientific tool used to measure temperature. Temperature is measured in degrees Celsius or Fahrenheit.

To read a thermometer, hold it so that the liquid is at eye level. Find the biggest number near the line of liquid. Then, estimate the temperature.

Ice skating means the lake is frozen solid—brrr!

How Hot? How Cold?

These thermometers show the temperatures at the lake.
Draw a line connecting each thermometer with the correct picture.

This thermometer says it is about 26 degrees Celsius.

This thermometer says it is about −6 degrees Celsius.

Sum It Up!

When you're done, use the answer key to check
and revise your work.

Write the vocabulary term that completes each caption.

1

The skis are long, hard, and
brightly-colored. These
traits are some of the skis'

_____.

2

The thermometer
measures how hot or
cold the surrounding air
is, or the air's

_____.

3

To measure the

_____ of
the bean, use a metric
ruler or tape measure.

Answer Key: 1. physical properties 2. temperature 3. length

Word Play

1 Draw a line from the word on the left to its definition on the right.

1. matter

2. physical property

3. length

4. millimeter

5. estimate

6. mass

7. gram

8. pan balance

9. temperature

a. the distance between two points

b. a unit of measure of mass

c. to make an educated guess

d. anything that takes up space and has mass

e. a tenth of a centimeter

f. a measurement of how hot or cold a solid, liquid, or gas is

g. how much matter is inside an object

h. a tool used to measure mass

i. something that tells us about matter

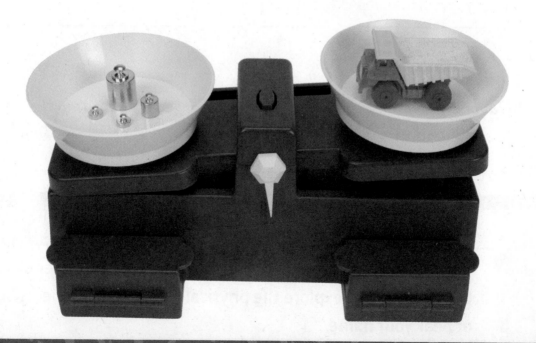

Apply Concepts

2 Describe the tool you would use to compare the beaks of these two birds.

_____

_____

_____

3 What physical property is measured in number 2, above?

_____

4 Katie is classifying items she's found along the shore. In her notebook, she has written a list to describe a stone. Place the letter _P_ next to each of Katie's observations that identify the stone's physical properties.

It is black.

It was found in the water.

It is hard.

_____

_____

_____

It is about 5 centimeters in diameter.

It sinks when dropped in water.

It fits in the palm of my hand.

_____

_____

_____

Take It Home! With a family member, use tools such as a thermometer or tape measure to explore the physical properties of objects in or near your home.

3.4.1 Choose and use the appropriate tools to estimate and measure length, mass and temperature in SI units.
Nature of Science

Name _____

Essential Question

What Tools and Units Can You Use to Measure?

Set a Purpose
What will you learn from this experiment?

_____

_____

_____

Think About the Procedure
What physical properties will you measure?

_____

_____

_____

_____

How will you use the tools to measure?

_____

_____

_____

_____

_____

_____

Record Your Data
In the space below, make a table that shows your results.

Draw Conclusions

Why do you think it is important to develop good measuring skills?

_____

_____

_____

_____

_____

Analyze and Extend

1. What do you think people use measurements for? When might it be important to know an object's length, mass, or temperature?

_____

_____

_____

_____

_____

2. How can you use the data you collected to classify the objects?

_____

_____

_____

_____

3. Think about other things you would like to ask about measurement. Record your thoughts in your science notebook.

_____

_____

_____

_____

_____

_____

The Design Process As citizens of the constructed world, students will participate in the design process. Students will learn to use materials and tools safely and employ the basic principles of the engineering design process in order to find solutions to problems.

Lesson 3

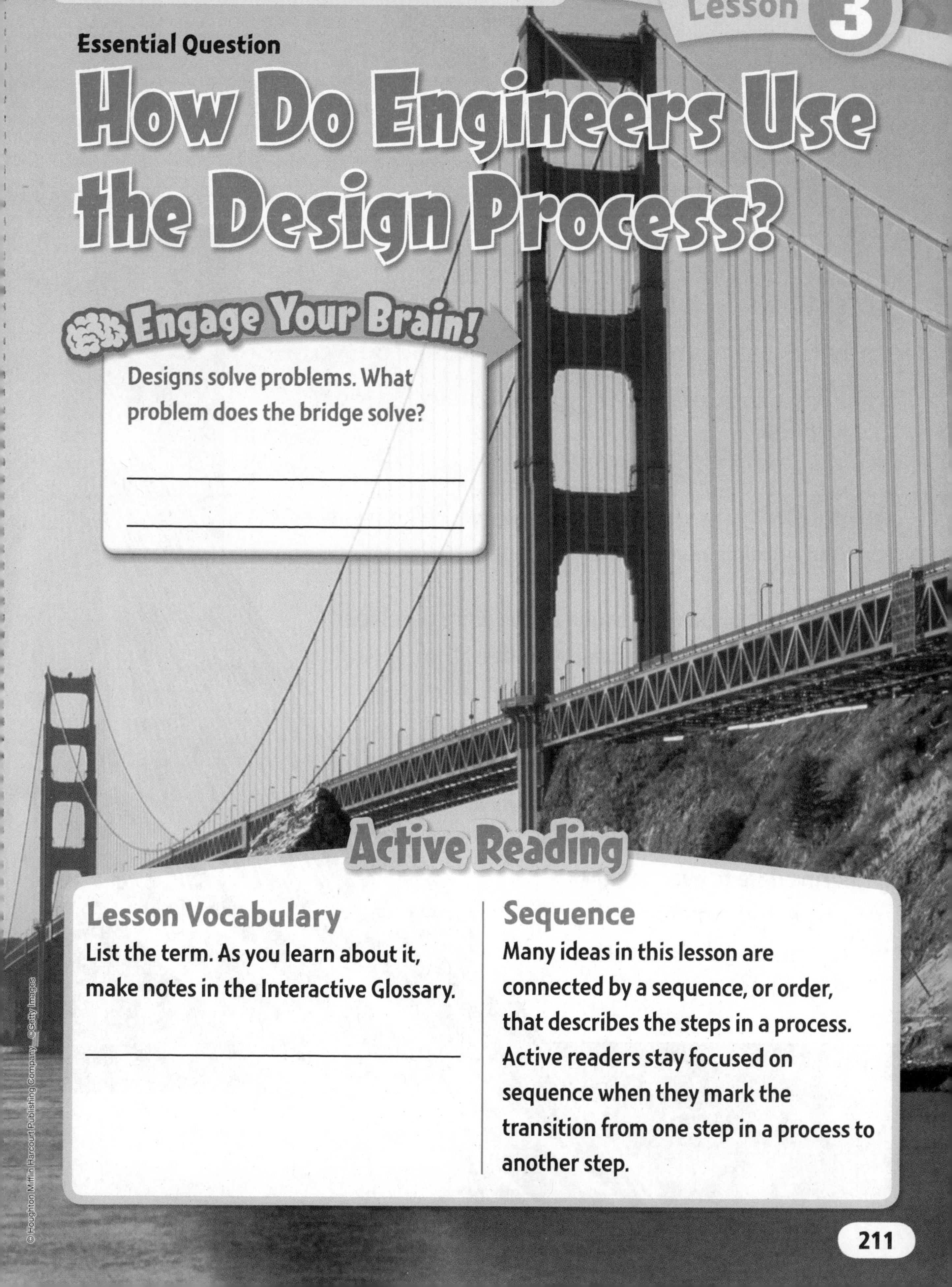

Essential Question

How Do Engineers Use the Design Process?

Engage Your Brain!

Designs solve problems. What problem does the bridge solve?

____

____

Active Reading

Lesson Vocabulary

List the term. As you learn about it, make notes in the Interactive Glossary.

____

Sequence

Many ideas in this lesson are connected by a sequence, or order, that describes the steps in a process. Active readers stay focused on sequence when they mark the transition from one step in a process to another step.

The Design Process

To get to school, you may have ridden your bike or taken the bus. These are two different ways of getting to school, they have something in common.

Active Reading As you read these two pages, write a number and then circle the number of the step in the design process.

Both methods of transportation above were developed by someone who used the design process. The **design process** is the process engineers follow to solve problems. It is a multi-step process that includes finding a problem and brainstorming ideas, keeping good records of your work, planning and building a prototype, gathering data to evaluate the prototype, and communicating the solution, testing data, and your improvements.

The William H. Natcher Bridge makes crossing the Ohio River easy and fast!

An engineer used the design process to design the supports for this bridge.

The design process can help people solve problems or design creative solutions. Look at the picture of the Ohio River between Rockport, Indiana, and Owensboro, Kentucky. In the past, there was only one bridge connecting these cities. Over time, it got very crowded. In this lesson, you'll see how the design process was used to design a solution to this problem.

How Do Inventions Help You?

Think of an invention that has made your life easier. What problem did it solve? How do you think its inventor used the design process to find the solution?

_____

_____

_____

_____

_____

Identifying the Problem

The design process starts with finding a problem and brainstorming ideas. An engineer can't design a solution without first knowing what the problem is!

Active Reading As you read these two pages, put brackets [ ] around the sentences that describe the problem and write P in front of the brackets. Put brackets around the sentences that describe the steps toward a solution and write S in front of the brackets.

A team of scientists and engineers worked together. They saw there was a lot of traffic on the old bridge. People of both cities needed another way to cross the Ohio River. The team studied the best way to get the most people and cars across the river. Then they brainstormed possible solutions.

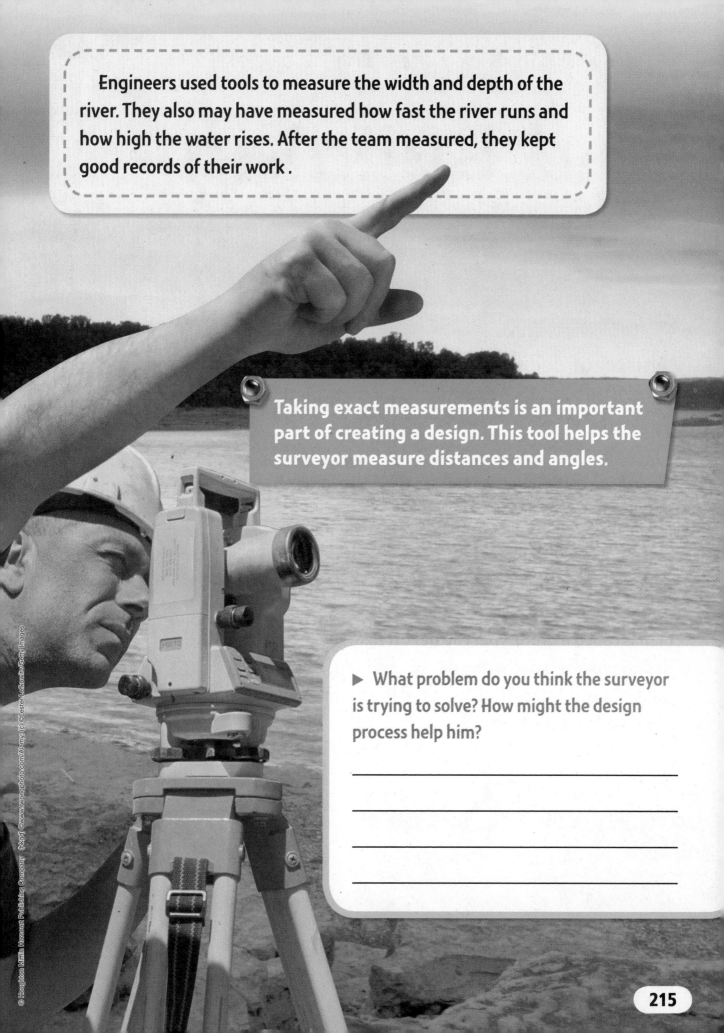

Engineers used tools to measure the width and depth of the river. They also may have measured how fast the river runs and how high the water rises. After the team measured, they kept good records of their work .

Taking exact measurements is an important part of creating a design. This tool helps the surveyor measure distances and angles.

▶ What problem do you think the surveyor is trying to solve? How might the design process help him?

_____

_____

_____

_____

Planning and Building a Prototype

The team decided the best solution would be to build another bridge across the Ohio River.

Active Reading As you read these two pages, underline the sentences that describe steps in the design process.

The next step in the design process is planning. The team chose a site for the future bridge. Many people worked together to prepare a plan for the bridge using exact measurements. This type of plan is called a prototype. The next step in the design process is gathering data to evaluate, or judge, the prototype. Builders used the prototype when building the bridge.

The next step in the design process is evaluating how well the solution works. Engineers carefully evaluated and tested the safety of the William H. Natcher Bridge. They made sure that builders followed the plans and used the correct materials.

The last step in the design process is to communicate the solution. Bridge inspectors used their findings, or evidence, to write reports. They used mathematical representations, such as graphs, tables, and drawings, to explain that the bridge was safe to open. Engineers could now use this information to make improvements and build bridges in other places!

The prototype helped builders know how wide, tall, and long to make the bridge.

Communication Is Key!

List three other ways you might communicate the results of a project to others.

_____

_____

How Do Engineers Improve a Design?

An engineer's work is never done! Every invention can be improved. For example, instead of building a fire in a wood stove or turning on a gas or electric oven, you can use a microwave to heat up your food.

Just as with stoves, engineers have come up with newer and better designs for cell phones. Forty years ago, cell phones were bulky and heavy. Today, the smallest cell phone is not much bigger than a watch!

Martin Cooper invented the first cell phone in 1973. It was 13 inches long, weighed about 2 pounds, and allowed only 30 minutes of talk time.

▶ What might happen if cell phones get too small?

_____

_____

_____

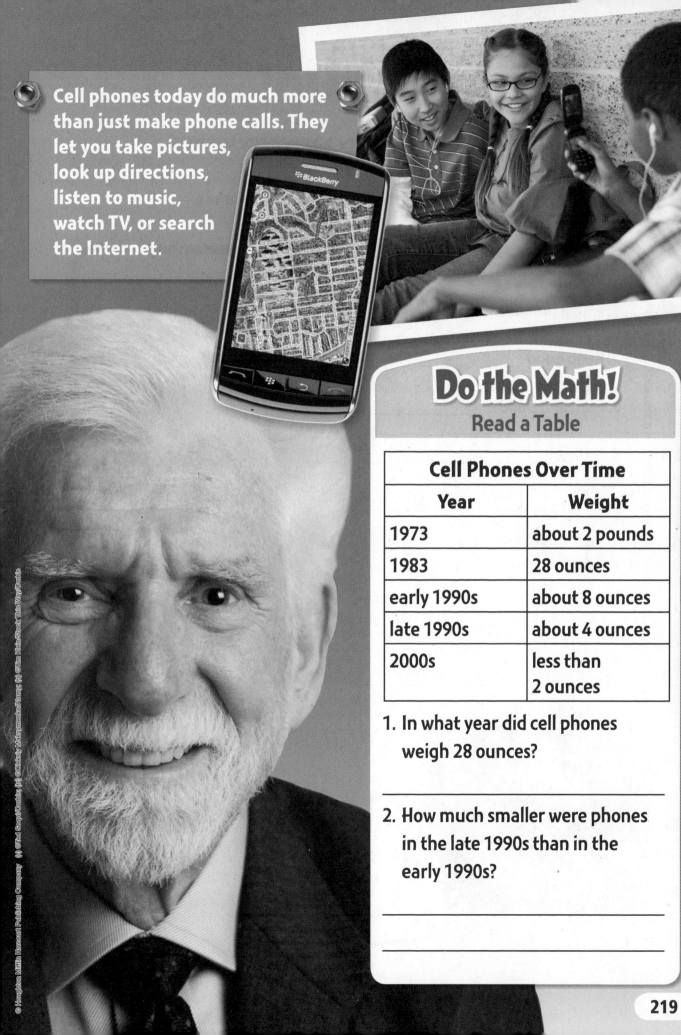

Cell phones today do much more than just make phone calls. They let you take pictures, look up directions, listen to music, watch TV, or search the Internet.

Do the Math!

Read a Table

Cell Phones Over Time	
Year	**Weight**
1973	about 2 pounds
1983	28 ounces
early 1990s	about 8 ounces
late 1990s	about 4 ounces
2000s	less than 2 ounces

1. In what year did cell phones weigh 28 ounces?

_____

2. How much smaller were phones in the late 1990s than in the early 1990s?

_____

_____

Sum It Up!

When you're done, use the answer key to check and revise your work.

Complete the step of the design process in each sentence.

1

1. Find a problem and _____ ideas.

2. Keep good _____ of your work.

3. Plan and build a _____.

4. Gather _____ to evaluate the prototype.

5. _____ the solution, test data, and your improvements.

Answer Key: 1. brainstorm; 2. records; 3. prototype; 4. data; 5. Communicate

Brain Check

Name _____

Word Play

1 Use these words to complete the puzzle.

Across

2. A plan for a solution that may use many drawings

6. A way of letting people know about a design

Down

1. Something that needs a solution

3. The steps engineers follow to solve problems

4. To judge how well a design works

5. The outcome of the design process

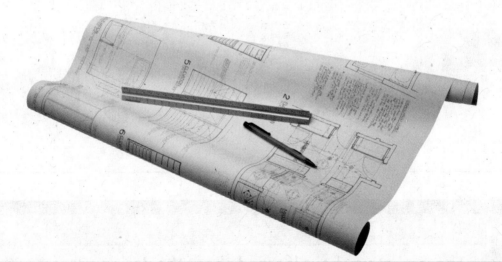

problem   process   solution   design   evaluate   communicate

Apply Concepts

2 Kyle's pet hamster is curious! It always finds a way out of its cage. Use the design process to help Kyle solve this problem.

_____

_____

_____

_____

_____

3 Label each of the following as a problem or solution.

_____ _____ _____ _____

Take It Home!

Share what you have learned about the design process with your family. With a family member, identify products that are good examples of the design process. What problems do they solve?

Careers in Science

1

Civil engineers plan the structures that are built in cities and towns. Roads and bridges are some of the things they plan.

2

The projects that civil engineers build need to be safe. They must hold up to daily use.

3

Civil engineers improve how we live. They help people get the things they need.

4

Civil engineers are important to a growing city or town. They look at the need for new structures.

8 Things YOU SHOULD KNOW ABOUT Civil Engineers

5

Civil engineers keep cars and trucks moving. They fix roads that are no longer safe.

6

Civil engineers make drawings called construction plans.

7

Civil engineers use tools, such as compasses and rulers. Many engineers use computers.

8

Some civil engineers measure the surface of the land. They use this data to plan buildings.

Engineering Emergency!

Match the problems that can be solved by a civil engineer with its solution in the illustration. Write the number of the problem in the correct triangle on the picture.

1 We have an energy shortage! We can harness the river's energy to generate electricity.

2 The city is getting crowded! More people are moving here. They need more places to live and work.

3 The streets are always jammed. We have a transportation crisis!

4 The nearest bridge is too far away. We need a faster and easier way to get across the river.

Think About It!

If you were a civil engineer, what kind of changes would you make where you live?

_____

_____

Essential Question

How Can You Use Simple Machines?

Engage Your Brain!

The skater looks like she's simply having fun, but she's also doing work. What work is being done? What simple machine do you think she is using?

_____

_____

_____

Active Reading

Lesson Vocabulary

List the terms. As you learn about each, make notes in the Interactive Glossary.

_____ _____

_____ _____

_____ _____

_____ _____

Problem and Solution

Ideas in this lesson may be connected by a problem-solution relationship. Active readers stay focused on problem-solution relationships when they ask themselves, What is the problem? How is the problem solved?

How Can We Use Simple Machines?

Think of the work you do each day. You do schoolwork. You may do other jobs at home, as well. By the time bedtime rolls around, you probably feel like you put in a full day's work!

Active Reading As you read these two pages, circle the word that has a different meaning in science.

Though it looks like play, moving sand with a shovel is also work.

Simple machines make it easier to do the work of pulling beach gear up a hill.

Inclined plane

Scientists define *work* in a different way. **Work** is the use of a force—a push or a pull—to move an object across a distance. Look at the children in the photographs. Digging in sand uses force to move the sand. Pulling beach gear up a hill uses force, too.

Both children are using simple machines to help them do the work. A **simple machine** has few or no moving parts. To use it, you apply only one force. The boy is using a shovel. The girl is using an inclined plane, a flat, sloping surface that makes moving and lifting things easier.

▶ Make a list of work you have done today. Hint: Work is the use of a push or pull to move an object.

_____

_____

_____

_____

_____

_____

_____

How Do Wedges and Levers Help You Do Work?

Simple machines help make work around the house easier. How do these machines work?

Active Reading As you read these two pages, find and underline the definitions of *wedge* and *lever*.

A **wedge** is made up of two inclined planes placed back to back. A knife is a type of wedge. A wedge is used to force two things apart or to split one thing into two. To move a wedge down through an object, you push the wedge down.

Wedge

As the woman pushes the knife blade into the celery, it splits into two pieces that move away from one another.

A **lever** is a bar that pivots on a fixed point. The fixed point is called the **fulcrum**. A fork is one kind of lever. The fulcrum is on one end. The lever's load—food on the fork—is at the other end. Force is applied by the fingers to hold up the food.

A seesaw is another kind of lever. Its fulcrum is in the middle. If your friend sits on one end of a seesaw, and you want to lift her from the ground, where will you apply force? You would sit on the other end of the seesaw. In this case, the fulcrum is the object on which the seesaw sits.

▶ Look at the two pictures on these pages. Identify the problem in each picture and explain how simple machines help solve it.

_____

_____

_____

_____

_____

_____

_____

The fork is not the only simple machine in this picture. The body has simple machines, too. The boy's teeth act as wedges, and the bones in his arm and hand are levers.

Lever

Fulcrum

How Do Pulleys and Wheels Help You Do Work?

Two kinds of simple machines use circular motion to make work easier.

Active Reading As you read these two pages, underline the words that signal a comparison is being made.

A **pulley** is a wheel with a rope, cord, or chain around it. It makes work easier by changing the direction of force.

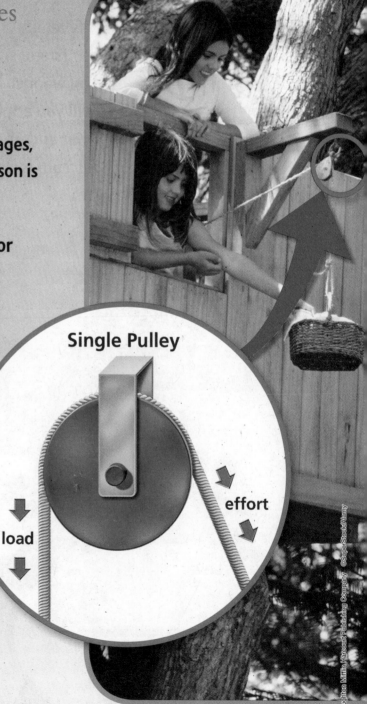

The pulley is attached to the tree house. It has a rope that runs around it and down to the ground. There, it is attached to a basket. Pulling the rope at the top makes the basket rise.

Single Pulley

load

effort

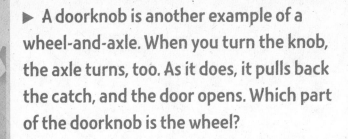

▶ A doorknob is another example of a wheel-and-axle. When you turn the knob, the axle turns, too. As it does, it pulls back the catch, and the door opens. Which part of the doorknob is the wheel?

_____

_____

The **wheel-and-axle** is made up of a wheel and an axle that are connected so they turn together. You know that a bicycle has wheels, and you might know that it has axles. But since the wheels and the axles of a bicycle aren't connected and don't turn together, they are not what a scientist would call a simple machine. However, the handlebars of the bicycle are a wheel-and-axle.

Turning the handlebar is like turning the blue wheel. The connected axle turns to steer the front bicycle wheel.

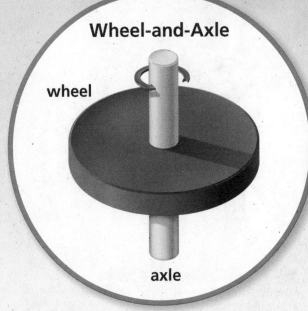

Wheel-and-Axle

wheel

axle

How Can Simple Machines Work Together?

Sometimes, two simple machines work together to get a job done. Which machines work this way?

Active Reading Draw triangles around the names of tools that are made of two simple machines working together.

Lever

Fulcrum

Wedge

The blades of the garden shears are wedges, and the handles are levers.

The garden trowel is also made up of a wedge and lever.

The garden shears are made up of two simple machines—a wedge and a lever. The blades of the shears are wedges. The handles are levers. When force is applied to one end, the blade end moves. The force you apply at the handles becomes a larger force that cuts the leaf from the stem.

Brainstorm!

What machines are made up of more than one simple machine?

_____

_____

_____

When you're done, use the answer key to check and revise your work.

Write the term that matches each picture and caption.

1
_____

This involves using force to move an object across a distance.

2

The fishing reel is made of two simple machines.

3
_____

You can use this simple machine to take a bite.

4

The slanted surface makes it easier for the skater to move across a distance.

5
_____

The lever balances on this.

Answer Key: 1. work; 2. pulley and lever; 3. wedge; 4. inclined plane; 5. fulcrum

Name _____

Word Play

1 Choose words from the box at the bottom to complete the word web. Then, add one detail about each item.

pulley   lever   inclined plane   simple machines   wheel-and-axle   wedge

Apply Concepts

2 Make a list of simple machines in your school.

_____

_____

_____

_____

_____

3 Label each simple machine.

  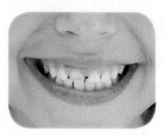 

_____ _____ _____ _____

_____ _____ _____

Take It Home!

Share what you have learned about simple machines with your family. With a family member, identify simple machines in your home. Discuss how they make work easier.

3.4.1 Choose and use the appropriate tools to estimate and measure length, mass and temperature in SI units. **3.4.2** Define the uses and types of simple machines and utilize simple machines in the solution to a real world problem. **Nature of Science, Design Process**

Name _____

Essential Question

How Can You Design a Tree House?

Set a Purpose

What parts of the design process will you use in this activity?

_____

_____

_____

_____

State Your Hypothesis

Write your hypothesis, or the idea you will test.

_____

_____

_____

_____

Think About the Procedure

Why is it important to think about how things move into and out of the tree house?

_____

_____

_____

_____

What problems do you identify? How can simple machines help you with these problems?

_____

_____

_____

_____

Record Your Data

In the space below, draw a design that needs simple machines to be built.

Draw Conclusions

Why do you think it was important to include simple machines in your design?

_____

_____

_____

Analyze and Extend

1. Suppose you were going to use the design process to build the tree house you've designed. What more would you need to do before you began building?

_____

_____

_____

2. What simple machines did you include? Why?

_____

_____

_____

_____

_____

_____

_____

3. Think about other things you would like to know about how the design process is used to plan projects like your tree house. Record your thoughts in your science notebook.

_____

_____

_____

_____

_____

_____

_____

Multiple Choice

Identify the choice that best answers the question.

3.4.1

1 You find that a cup with an ice cube in it has a mass of 42 grams. You measure the mass again just after the ice cube melts. What would the BEST estimate of the mass of the cup and the water from the melted ice cube?

(A) The mass would be 54 grams.

(B) The mass would be 45 grams.

(C) The mass would be 42 grams.

(D) The mass would be 38 grams.

3.4.1

2 You have two 20-cm metric rulers. One is made of metal, and the other is made of plastic. What would be the BEST way to show that they are made of different kinds of matter?

(A) You can compare their masses.

(B) You can compare their shapes.

(C) You can compare their lengths.

(D) You can compare their volumes.

3.4.1

3 Which measurement is the MOST accurate for the rose shown below?

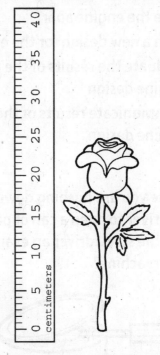

(A) The rose is about 27 inches tall.

(B) The rose is about 27 meters tall.

(C) The rose is about 27 millimeters tall.

(D) The rose is about 27 centimeters tall.

Design Process

4 What problem did adding air conditioning to cars solve?

(A) Car engines got too hot during the summer.

(B) People got too cold inside cars during the winter.

(C) People got too hot inside cars during the summer.

(D) The car radio got too hot during hot summer days.

Design Process

5 Scientists notice a problem with an engine. It is getting too hot after it runs for a long time. What should the scientists do NEXT?

(A) take the engine apart

(B) plan a new design for the engine

(C) evaluate the results of the new engine design

(D) communicate results of the new engine design

3.4.2

6 Suppose you are pushing down on a screwdriver to open a can of paint. How is the screwdriver an example of a simple machine?

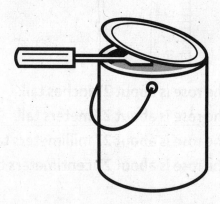

(A) It is a lever that changes the direction of the force needed to open the lid.

(B) It is a wedge that splits the lid from the can when pushed between them.

(C) It is a wheel-and-axle that opens the can by turning the screwdriver.

(D) It is a pulley. When you push down, the lid goes up.

Nature of Science

7 You have a box of colorful crayons. Which set of words BEST describes the crayons' physical properties?

(A) hard, colorful, waxy smell

(B) soft, fluffy, watery

(C) crayon, box, paper

(D) rough, large, loud

3.4.1

8 You want to compare how fast you can run with how fast your dog can run. Which of the following tools will you need?

(A) meter stick and pan balance

(B) thermometer and tape measure

(C) stopwatch and meter stick

(D) meter stick and tape measure

3.4.1

9 Your science partner collects data during your investigation. The data is 20 °C. What did your partner measure?

(A) the mass of an item

(B) the length of an item

(C) the space an item takes up

(D) the temperature of an item

Nature of Science

10 Here are the physical properties of an unknown object. It is about 15 cm long and 1 cm wide. It is hollow and shaped like a tube. It is made of plastic. It has a mass of less than 1 gram. What might the object be?

- Ⓐ a pencil
- Ⓑ a piece of pasta
- Ⓒ a drinking straw
- Ⓓ a paper towel tube

3.4.1, Nature of Science

11 Suppose boiling water was just poured into your cup and is too hot to drink. You wait until it cools and finally take a sip. You wonder how much the water cooled down before you could take a sip. How could you find out?

- Ⓐ You could wait until the water becomes cool and then take its temperature.
- Ⓑ You could pour the cool water into a beaker to see how much space it takes up.
- Ⓒ You could find the mass of the hot water and its mass again once it has cooled. Then subtract the two numbers to find the difference.
- Ⓓ You could take the temperature of the hot water and take the water's temperature again once it has cooled. Then subtract the two numbers to find the difference.

Design Process

12 An engineer designs a new engine, but one of the parts keeps melting. The engine can get hotter than 240 °C. Look at the table. Which material would you suggest the engineer use in the next design?

Material	Melting Point (°C)
Potassium	64
Plastic	120
Tin	232
Aluminum	660

- Ⓐ The engineer should use tin.
- Ⓑ The engineer should use plastic.
- Ⓒ The engineer should use aluminum.
- Ⓓ The engineer should use potassium.

Design Process

13 What is the MAIN goal of the design process?

- Ⓐ to find solutions to problems
- Ⓑ to make charts and graphs
- Ⓒ to write articles for magazines
- Ⓓ to give scientists something to do

3.4.2

14 Suppose you are digging a stone out of the ground with a shovel. The shovel is the lever. The place on the ground where the shovel touches is the fulcrum. Using the shovel, what do you need to do to move the rock?

- Ⓐ Pull the lever up.
- Ⓑ Push the lever down.
- Ⓒ Use your hands and pick up the rock.
- Ⓓ Move the fulcrum farther away from the rock.

3.4.2

15 According to scientists, which of the following describes work?

Ⓐ reading a book for homework

Ⓑ thinking of an answer to a math question

Ⓒ filling a bucket of sand while playing in a sandbox

Ⓓ watching a video in science class about simple machines

3.4.1

16 Which tool would be BEST to use if you want to measure the length of an ant as accurately as possible?

Ⓐ a 20-cm metric ruler showing only centimeters

Ⓑ a 20-cm metric ruler showing millimeters

Ⓒ a tape measure

Ⓓ a meter stick

3.4.1

17 A good estimate for the length of a car is 3 meters. Which is the BEST estimate for the length of your classroom?

Ⓐ 1 meter

Ⓑ 10 meters

Ⓒ 100 meters

Ⓓ 1000 meters

3.4.1

18 What is TRUE about the two items on the pan balance below?

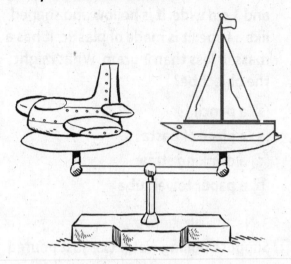

Ⓐ They have similar masses and physical properties.

Ⓑ They have similar masses but take up different amounts of space.

Ⓒ They have the same properties but take up different amounts of space.

Ⓓ They take up the same amount of space, but one has a much greater mass.

3.4.2

19 Suppose you are in a tree house and need to bring up a basket of toys. Which simple machine could you use?

Ⓐ a wedge

Ⓑ a wheel-and-axle

Ⓒ a pulley

Ⓓ a lever

3.4.2

20 You are riding on a seesaw at recess with a friend. You notice that if you move closer to the center of the seesaw it is harder to lift your friend. What do you need to do to lift your friend more easily?

(A) push down harder

(B) bounce up and down

(C) move closer to the fulcrum

(D) move away from the fulcrum

Constructed Response

Design Process

21 Below is a list of some of the steps in the design process. Write numbers next to the steps to show the correct order.

_____ Communicate the solution using graphs and data tables.

_____ Identify the problem to be solved.

_____ Test and evaluate the solution.

_____ Brainstorm potential solutions.

Explain why it is important to communicate your solution with others.

_____

_____

_____

3.4.2, Design Process

22 You move to a new home with a doghouse in the backyard. Your small dog cannot get into the doghouse easily because it is raised up off the ground.

What is the problem? What can you do to solve the problem?

_____

_____

_____

Which simple machines would you use?

_____

3.4.1

23 The drawing below shows a bowling ball, soccer ball, and baseball.

Which physical properties are the same? Which physical properties are different?

_____

_____

_____

How could you use tools to measure the differences?

_____

_____

Extended Response

3.4.1, Nature of Science

24 It is a sunny day, and you are very hot in your wool sweater. You wonder if you would have been more comfortable wearing a cotton sweatshirt instead.

What test can you make to answer your question?

_____

_____

What tools could you use to measure the results?

_____

_____

Predict what may happen in your test.

_____

_____

3.4.1, Design Process

25 Your class is doing an investigation to see which design of paper airplane flies the farthest. Your class brainstormed and agreed on the three designs shown below. Each design was flown 3 times. The result for each trial is recorded in the data table.

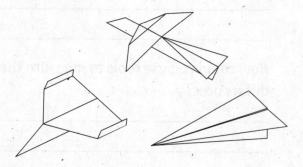

Data Table

Flight	Design 1 results	Design 2 results	Design 3 results
1	240 cm	78 cm	293 cm
2	198 cm	102 cm	302 cm
3	236 cm	122 cm	252 cm

How did students make the airplanes?

_____

_____

_____

How did they collect the data? Which tools did they use?

_____

_____

_____

Which design flew the farthest? How do you know?

_____

_____

What could be done if the students wanted a paper airplane to go even farther?

_____

_____

_____

Interactive Glossary

As you learn about each term, add notes, drawings, or sentences in the extra space. This will help you remember what the terms mean. Here are some examples.

fungi [FUHN•jee] A group of organisms that get nutrients by decomposing other organisms.

A mushroom is an example of fungi.

physical change [FIHZ•ih•kuhl CHAYNJ] Change in the size, shape, or state of matter with no new substance being formed.

When I cut paper in half, that's a physical change.

Glossary Pronunciation Key

With every glossary term, there is also a phonetic respelling. A phonetic respelling writes the word the way it sounds, which can help you pronounce new or unfamiliar words. Use this key to help you understand the respellings.

Sound	As in	Phonetic Respelling	Sound	As in	Phonetic Respelling
a	bat	(BAT)	oh	over	(OH•ver)
ah	lock	(LAHK)	oo	pool	(POOL)
air	rare	(RAIR)	ow	out	(OWT)
ar	argue	(AR•gyoo)	oy	foil	(FOYL)
aw	law	(LAW)	s	cell	(SEL)
ay	face	(FAYS)		sit	(SIT)
ch	chapel	(CHAP•uhl)	sh	sheep	(SHEEP)
e	test	(TEST)	th	that	(THAT)
	metric	(MEH•trik)		thin	(THIN)
ee	eat	(EET)	u	pull	(PUL)
	feet	(FEET)	uh	medal	(MED•uhl)
	ski	(SKEE)		talent	(TAL•uhnt)
er	paper	(PAY•per)		pencil	(PEN•suhl)
	fern	(FERN)		onion	(UHN•yuhn)
eye	idea	(eye•DEE•uh)		playful	(PLAY•fuhl)
i	bit	(BIT)		dull	(DUHL)
ing	going	(GOH•ing)	y	yes	(YES)
k	card	(KARD)		ripe	(RYP)
	kite	(KYT)	z	bags	(BAGZ)
ngk	bank	(BANGK)	zh	treasure	(TREZH•er)

Interactive Glossary

A

absorb [ab•SAWRB] Take in by an object (p. 93)

B

bar graph [BAHR GRAF] A graph using parallel bars of varying lengths to show comparison (p. 37)

C

chart [CHART] A display that organizes data into rows and columns (p. 37)

cone [KOHN] A part of some nonflowering plants where seeds form (p. 167)

conserve [kuhn•SURV] To use less of something to make it last longer (p. 143)

D

data [DEY•tuh] Individual facts, statistics, and items of information (p. 35)

data table [DEY•tuh TEY•buhl] A set of rows and columns used to record data from investigations (p. 37)

design process [dih•ZYN PROS•es] The process of applying basic principles of engineering to solve problems (p. 212)

experiment [ek•SPAIR•uh•muhnt] A test done to see if a hypothesis is correct or not (p. 211)

E

energy [EN•er•jee] The ability to make something move or change (p. 58)

extinct [ex•STINGT] No longer existing or living (p. 130)

environment [en•VY•ruhn•muhnt] The things, both living and nonliving, that surround a living thing (p. 176)

F

flower [FLOW•er] The part of a flowering plant that enables it to reproduce (p. 166)

evidence [EV•uh•duhns] Information, collected during an investigation, to support a hypothesis (p. 35)

fossil [FAHS•uhl] The remains or traces of a plant or animal that lived long ago (p. 130) fulcrum [FUHL•kruhm] The balance point on a lever that supports the arm but does not move (p. 229)

G

germinate [JER•muh•nayt] To start to grow (a seed) (p. 178)

graduated cylinder [GRAJ•oo•ay•tid SIL•in•der] A container marked with a graded scale used for measuring liquids (p. 21)

gram [GRAM] A measurement of mass or the amount of matter in an object (p. 200)

H

hypothesis [hy•PAHTH•uh•sis] A possible answer to a question that can be tested to see if it is correct (p. 10)

I

infer [in•FER] To draw a conclusion about something (p. 6)

investigation [in•ves•tuh•GAY•shuhn] A study that a scientist does (p. 9)

L

length [LENGKTH] A measurement of distance between two points (p. 198)

lever [LEV•er] A simple machine made up of a bar that pivots, or turns, on a fixed point (p. 229)

M

map [MAP] A picture that shows the locations of things (p. 37)

mass [MAS] The amount of matter in an object (p. 200)

matter [MAT•er] Anything that takes up space (p. 197)

microscope [MY•kruh•skohp] A tool that makes an object look several times bigger than it is (p. 19)

millimeter [MIL•uh•mee•ter] A unit of measurement in the metric system equal to one tenth of a centimeter (p. 199)

mineral [MIN•er•uhl] A nonliving solid that has a crystal form (p. 114)

nonrenewable resource [nahn•rih•NOO•uh•buhl REE•sawrs] A resource that, once used, cannot be replaced in a reasonable amount of time (p. 142)

model [MOD•l] Something used to represent anything that cannot be easily studied (p. 36)

nutrient [NOO•tree•uhnt] The parts of the soil that help plants grow and stay healthy (p. 160)

N

natural resource [NACH•er•uhl REE•sawrs] Anything from nature that people can use (p. 141)

O

observe [uhb•ZURV] To use your senses to gather information (p. 6)

P

pan balance [PAN BEL•uhns] A tool that measures mass (p. 202)

physical property [FIZ•ih•kuhl PRAHP•er•tee] Anything that you can observe about an object by using one or more of your senses (p. 197)

pulley [PUHL•ee] A simple machine made of a wheel with a rope, cord, or chain around it (p. 230)

R

pitch [PICH] How high or low a sound is (p. 63)

reflect [rih•FLEKT] To bounce off (p. 94)

refract [rih•FRAKT] To bend light as it moves from one material to another (p. 96)

predict [pri•DIKT] Use observations and data to form an idea of what will happen under certain conditions (p. 8)

renewable resource [rih•NOO•uh•buhl REE•sawrs] A resource that can be replaced within a reasonable amount of time (p. 141)

Interactive Glossary

reproduce [ree•pruh•DOOS] To make more living things of the same kind (p. 166)

shadow [SHAD•oh] A dark area that forms when an object blocks the path of light (p. 93)

rock [RAHK] A naturally formed solid made of one or more minerals (p. 120)

simple machine [SIM•puhl muh•SHEEN] A machine with few or no moving parts that needs only one force applied (p. 227)

S

seed [SEED] A structure that contains a young plant and its food supply, surrounded by a protective coat (p. 166)

sound [SOWND] Energy you can hear (p. 58)

sound wave [SOWND WAYV] Vibrations moving through matter (p. 75)

T

temperature [TEM•per•uh•cher] A measure of how hot or cold something is (pp. 23, 205)

thermometer [ther•MAHM•uht•ter] A tool used to measure temperature (p. 205)

V

variable [VAIR•ee•uh•buhl] The one thing that changes in an experiment (p. 11)

vibrate [VY•brayt] To move back and forth very quickly (p. 60)

W

wedge [WEJ] A simple machine composed of two inclined planes back to back (p. 228)

wheel-and-axle [WEEL AND AK•suhl] A simple machine made of a wheel and an axle that turn together (p. 231)

work [WERK] The use of a force to move an object across a distance (p. 227)

© Houghton Mifflin Harcourt Publishing Company

Index

Index

movement, 92, 103–104

plants growing toward, 176–177, 182, 185–186

reflection, 94–95

refraction, 96–97

traveling in straight path, 92–93, 100

Light beam, 92

Light microscope, 18–19

Lightning, 58–59

Limestone, 117, 124, 143

Liquid, 205

particles in, 79

sound traveling through, 78–79

Luster (of minerals), 118, 123

earthy, 119, 124

glassy, 119

metallic, 118–119, 122, 124

talc and gypsum, 118

M

Ma, Lena Qiying, 149

Magnetite, 120, 123

Magnifying box, 28

Main Idea and Details, 4, 20, 33, 36, 42, 58, 73, 78, 129, 139–140, 162, 175–176, 180, 182

Mammals

dolphin, 79

hamster, 222

whale, 73

Marengo Cave, Indiana, 111

Mass, 21, 200–201, 207, 209–210

measuring, 202–203

Mathematics Skills. *See* **Do the Math!**

Matter, 196–197, 205, 207

Measure, 20, 24–25, 29–30, 47, 149, 173, 198–203, 205–210, 214–216

balance, 26–27

draw conclusions, 30

length, 21, 26

mass, 21, 202–203

temperature, 23

time, 22, 26

volume, 21

Measuring cup, 21. *See also* **Science tools**

Measuring spoon, 21, 28. *See also* **Science tools**

Measuring tape, 20, 28. *See also* **Science tools**

Metallic luster, 118–119, 122, 124

Metamorphic rock, 117

Meteorologist, 47–48

Microscope, 2, 18, 26, 99. *See also* **Science tools**

object magnification, 19

Millimeter, 199, 207

Minerals, 113–115, 145. *See also* **Rock**

break down, 120–123

calcite, 115, 121, 124

cleavage, 120–123

colors, 120–121

copper, 118, 123

corundum, 121

crystal, 115, 120–123

diamond, 113, 115, 118–119

elements, 115

fluorite, 115, 121–123

gold, 118, 122–123

graphite, 122

gypsum, 118

halite, 123

hardness, 118–119, 121–124

luster, 118–119, 122–124

magnetite, 120

mica, 121–122

properties of, 120–121, 125–126

pyrite, 115, 120, 123

quartz, 121, 124

rubies, 115, 125

scratch, 118–119

silver, 118, 123

streak colors, 120–123

talc, 118, 124

Mohs, Friedrich, 118

Mohs' hardness scale, 118, 124

Index

Index